Master the Property Game
How to Go from Debt to Financial Freedom

Damian Slominski
Shane Watson

MASTER THE PROPERTY GAME – HOW TO GO FROM DEBT TO FINANCIAL FREEDOM

Published by
10-10-10 Publishing
Markham, Ontario
CANADA

ISBN 13: 978-1530087433
Copyright © 2016 by Damian Slominski and Shane Watson
London, England, United Kingdom
www.masterthepropertygame.com
E: Info@masterthepropertygame.com

All Rights Reserved

No part of this book may be reproduced in any form, by photocopying or by electronic or mechanical means, including information storage or retrieval systems, without permission in writing from both the copyright owner and the publisher of this book. This book is not intended to give any legal, media, and/or financial advice to the readers.

For information about special discounts for bulk purchases, please contact 10-10-10 Publishing at 1-888-504-6257

Printed in the United Kingdom

Contents

Foreword	vii
About the Authors	ix
Introduction	xxvii
Chapter I - Mindset	1
Chapter II - Property: The Fundamentals	17
Chapter III - Raising Finance	39
Chapter IV - How to Find Property Bargains	55
Chapter V - Cash Flow/Passive Income	59
Chapter VI - Lease Options/Rent to Buy	67
Chapter VII - HMO and Rent to Rent	79
Chapter VIII - Buy to Sell vs Buy to Let	87
Chapter IX - Auctions	97
Chapter X - Get Started and Master the Property Game	103
Acknowledgements	109

Dedication by Shane Watson

I would like to dedicate this book to my parents for instilling strict values in me consistently from a young age which I have taken with me throughout my life up until this day. As a youngster I used to wonder why but it was done for a good cause and that's the reason why I am the man I am today – they are true visionaries. Thank You.

Dedication by Damian Slominski

This book is dedicated to my parents, Bernadeta Slominska and Robert Slominski, for raising me, instilling traditional values and exposing me to business from a young age. Thank you both for giving me the strength and support to reach for the stars and chase my dreams. I would also like to thank you for listening and always being there for me the best you can. This has had a positive effect on my personal and business life.

Foreword

Have you ever thought about your life purpose? Like most people, you probably have not. Have you ever thought that it was time to transform your life, but never knew how? You probably have lots of things you love doing and many things you want to experience and goals you want to achieve, and you dream of an extraordinary life. Again, if you are like many people, your life is filled with activities, obligations and commitments that have nothing to do with your goals or your dreams. You may be spending your life running faster and faster trying to keep up, and at the same time falling further and further away from living that extraordinary life you dream of.

When we meet people who have transformed their life, they always seem more interesting, more engaging. They have a renewed energy, they are passionate about their work, about life and, in general, about everything. To transform your life takes time, passion, courage and a lot of self-awareness.

Damian and Shane are entrepreneurs from London, England. They have achieved a lot of success in property investing, and by the time they were 25 they became financially free. Their knowledge in property investing is first class. I was struck by how much they know, their willingness to share and their passion for property.

This book explains how to invest in property without using any of your own money. You will find very simple ideas, guidelines and suggestions on how to gain financial freedom in property to empower you to transform your life and start living the life you deserve. All you need to do is take action.

Raymond Aaron
Leading Transformational Success Mentor
New York Times Bestselling Author

About the Authors

Damian Slominski

When I was 5 years old, I received a Christmas present. It was one that every kid dreamed about at my age – a pedal car with lights charged by a little battery. I was a happy kid! I was born in Poland, and lived in a village with my parents and sister at my grandparents' house. My dad at that time had his own company distributing gas in all the local villages. When I was a kid, I always wanted to copy my dad and become an entrepreneur, as he was a role model to me.

I was 5 years old and had everything I needed to start a business and be like my dad. My grandfather made me a little trailer to attach to my little car. He had a farm, and was doing everything by himself. He was a handyman and knew how to do everything. He brought a lot of wood from the forest and chopped it into small pieces. Because I wanted to be like my dad, I put as much wood as I could into my little trailer, attached it to my pedal car and started selling it to the neighbours in the village. Of course, nobody could say no to a 5-year-old kid. I started making money at a very young age.

When we are kids we always try to copy our parents, and people who surround us, because we trust them and believe that they are the right role models. Sometimes we soak in the right information, and sometimes the wrong if they tell us that we are not good enough. We may code it into our brains, potentially blocking us for the rest of our lives, believing we are not good and can never achieve anything. I was programmed by my dad to become an entrepreneur because he was one of them. I think I was lucky to be taught that way. If he was working for someone, it's likely I would have wanted to follow him and work for somebody else too.

Even if you were taught to be a worker, you can always reprogram yourself at a later stage; the only difference is that you will have to go through the hard times before you notice. If you want to be a millionaire it is nearly impossible or very hard to achieve it by working for someone 9-5 unless you are a CEO of a company like Apple or Microsoft. I am not saying that being an entrepreneur is easier than working for somebody else; sometimes it's much harder, but at least you are building your own business and making money for you. You are building an asset that you can eventually sell one day, you can't sell your position working for someone else or pass it to your kids – it doesn't work this way. Worst case scenario: you could be made redundant at any time. Starting your own business is a risk but working for someone that could fire you at any time is even more risky.

That is why it is very important to teach our kids about business at an early age so they don't work hard for a job to eventually find it's not the way they want to live; paying higher taxes than the rich; making money just to pay your bills and live pay check to pay check, month after month. Business is a journey, it's a learning curve, and sometimes you have to fail a few times before you achieve success. That is just the way it is – we learn by making mistakes. People think that success is a straight line to the top. I can tell you now it's not! My dad failed in business many times, and I did too. There were mud, tears and struggle. I am only 25 years old when writing this but I went through a lot of tough times to get where I am now.

Today, my business partner, Shane, and I are both financially free. We have a lot of properties all over the UK that we own and control. We don't have to do any physical work; we get passive income while we sleep 24 hours non-stop. Property gave us the freedom to do whatever we want in our lives; if we decide to go on holidays for 3 months, we can go without having to worry about money or business because everything is systemised and the money comes to our bank account every single month. But it wasn't always that good.

When I was 15/16 years old, I finished school in Poland and we moved to the UK. That was a big change, to go from living in a village to moving into a big city like London. I never thought that I would move to a different country. I was very excited, as it was a big opportunity for me to play football professionally. I wanted to become a footballer so I could make a lot of money and invest it into assets. As we know, England has the best football clubs in the world and it is everyone's dream to play for a Premier League club. I tried everything I could to fulfil my dream. I was in a football academy in a very well-known college. I went for trials at West Ham United, Leyton Orient and Polish Premier League club Lech Poznan. Unfortunately, I didn't make it and never became a professional footballer.

When I came to the UK, I couldn't speak a single word of English. It isn't easy to learn biology, chemistry or physics in a different language, especially if you can't even say "how are you?" The head teacher offered me extra English lessons during my breaks and gaps that I had in a day. I had a very nice teacher called Jackie, who helped me with the language barrier, and she even stayed at every single lesson to help me translate everything. While learning the language, I played football in college, for local clubs and I also started doing private gardening jobs: cutting grass, trimming hedges, planting etc. I got all the jobs from my mum as she had a cleaning company and people asked her if she knew anyone that could do their gardens. She knew that I was hard-working and she mentioned me. I started the first garden and needed some tools so my dad bought them for me. I soon had more and more clients. I started distributing leaflets and eventually I had so much interest that I sometimes had to say no. The only problem was that I was so busy with gardening and playing football after college and I couldn't find time to enjoy the money. It took me a couple of years to figure out that business is not about working in the business, it is about leveraging the time and working on the business by hiring people to do the work for you so you can focus on something else. I think this was the one puzzle that my dad forgot to teach me and that was the most important element. He had many employees but he was also working in his business all the time instead of systemising it properly and moving on to start a new business.

I managed to finish college and went to university. By that time I could speak English well. I still played football and chased my dream and did gardening so I didn't have to borrow any money from my parents for travel, car insurance and other expenses. But with gardening, it wasn't as easy to make money and having as many customers as I had during my college times because recession kicked in and I lost more than half of the customers. They couldn't afford a gardener any more, I assumed.

In the second year of university, I had lost even more customers and I decided to find a part-time job as a van driver for a charity. I wasn't taught to go and work for someone but life doesn't always go to plan. I didn't want to take money from my parents for my expenses so I decided to find a job. I was working there until I graduated from university. I had to quit because there was an incident whereby two of us were delivering a piano and I pulled the muscles in my back. I woke up at 3 am, wanting to go to the toilet and I couldn't get up or even move on the side. I had to call the ambulance. It wasn't a good idea to put my health in jeopardy by working so hard for somebody else.

I finished university and had no job but I had a lot of money saved in my bank account, so I decided to contact a friend that I met in a club three years prior. I met him regularly and he told me about his business interests. I invested a lot of money, at the time, into one of his businesses. He had a beauty pageant company organising events every year and choosing a Beauty Queen for the particular area in the UK. I was supposed to get 2x as much return on my money. The event happened and I attended, but I have never received any money back from him. Everything was contracted and signed but later on I found out that his company was constantly dormant so I couldn't even go to court and sue him. It was a failure for me and a lesson to avoid in the future: do your due diligence, before you get involved in any business!

This was the lowest point of my life as I had lost all the money that I saved whilst working very hard and got into debt on my credit card. I didn't have much choice and I had to take a job in a big shopping centre doing cleaning. They wanted me to clean the same windows every single day, constantly promising that I will get promoted. It was also a night shift job and I found it hard to adapt to the lifestyle. I was always tired. After 6 weeks, I said to myself: "What the hell am I doing?" I left that job, paid off my credit card and started doing gardening again to save some money for my next business.

This time I decided to open an online shop with flowers. Somebody told me that it was a very good business, especially around Valentine's Day and Mother's Day. I did my research and found whatever information I could about where to buy flowers, how to look after them so they last and how to protect them during transportation etc. I spent a lot of money on the website, all the equipment and flower boxes. I launched it around Valentine's Day. It was very exciting and I was looking forward to it hoping to sell 100s of bouquets. However, the web designer made a mistake: the checkout wasn't working properly. I was losing sales. He managed to fix it quickly but I already lost a lot of money on marketing. Altogether I managed to make 70 sales in 2 days. My mum helped me put up the bouquets and got it shipped to customers. It was a nightmare doing this amount in such a short amount of time. I made a mistake again by doing nearly everything by myself instead of hiring people to do it for me and leveraging time. The web designer managed my Google ad words campaign and wanted me to compete with the big companies by paying £2 per click, which was the biggest mistake I made. I lost much more money than I earned and it was a failure for me again. Everyone was telling me that whatever money I invested in any business, I always lost. I had the online florist for a couple more months, but after the Valentine's Day episode, nothing changed and I had debt on credit cards again.

After, I found a part-time job as a van driver delivering groceries for a big supermarket just to pay my bills and credit cards while looking for new business opportunities. I felt that I was not good at doing business and I was really disappointed, especially when people who were very close to me put me down too. They asked me when I was going to find a normal job like everyone else. I still remember those words. They said to me "Stop dreaming!" "You need money first to start making money! Wake up! You will need to find a job one day anyway!" Although this was a low point for me, I never agreed with what they said. Some of my family still don't even know that I invest in property and that I am financially free or do not need to work for somebody else anymore. They think that I sit at home and do nothing. If they feel better thinking about me that way, good for them as it doesn't bother me much.

Whilst working as a delivery driver, I decided not to give up on my dreams. While surfing on the internet, I found an ad saying that someone was organising an event teaching people how to buy properties without using any of their own money. It sounded too good to be true, but I decided to give it a try and I signed up because it was free. My mum was already a property investor making good money from properties without needing to work for it and I also had my first property at the age of 18 that was making some money. I noticed that from all businesses I had tried before, this was the only one making a regular income and positive cash flow.

The 3 day property event I attended, for free, completely changed my life. I was blown away with what I learnt but there was still a lot more to find out, and they offered another course that came with one-year mentoring that cost a lot of money. I really wanted to do it but I didn't have the money to pay for it. I had a few credit cards with some available balance. I applied for more cards and raised a limit on my old ones and somehow I managed to pay for the mentoring and I've never looked back.

I left my part-time job within a few months' time. There is nothing better than investing in yourself because once you have the knowledge, you will know how to make money even without having any money. Knowledge is power and nobody can take it away from you. During that 3 day event, I also met my business partner Shane, which was the best thing that could have happened to me as we are still working together and have achieved a lot of success. The course helped us to gain more properties and achieve financial freedom, so we can now teach others how to achieve the same results and change their life.

Shane Watson

I came from very humble beginnings. My father was, and is still, a lorry driver and my mother has worked in the job centre for the last 16 years. They never indulged in any kind of business activities and definitely were not property investors. I grew up firstly in the borough of Newham and then in my late teens moved to Croydon. My parents were always there for me and always provided for me, my brother and two sisters. My father sometimes flirted with the idea of going into business when I was young but it didn't really materialise.

My father worked hard to provide for the family and after my parents split when I was 13 years of age that didn't change. Even though we didn't have it all - I mean I never went abroad until I was 18 and I never had the newest trainers like most of my friends or the latest video games. Yes, there were many difficult times but I wouldn't change my childhood for the world as it has shaped me into the man I am today. One thing that was also consistent throughout my childhood was my father's strict ways. As the oldest, I was always reminded that it is extremely important to set a good example for my younger siblings. I had rules to follow and daily chores to upkeep and, if they were abided by, I would be rewarded with pocket money at the end of every month. I was taught the true value of hard work, taking responsibility and being consistent.

Growing up I was always told to get an education and that getting good grades at school would be the key to success in life. I was taught this at home and in school. Despite this, I still left school with poor GCSE grades. I remember how nervous I was opening that envelope; my heart was in my mouth, and then the empty sinking feeling I had when I only saw three C grades. I was hurt and left in a hurry before anyone else would ask me how I had done.

After being down in the dumps for a few days, and after the encouragement from my dad and step mum, I picked myself up and applied for college. I chose to go into construction and applied for a two year programme in Electrical Installation. I was so excited as this was a new beginning for me; a new-found hope. After a shaky start, I took to electrical installation like a duck to water and I was in the top 3 out of a group of 30. At the end of the first year the class was cut down from 30 to 15 and I was selected to go onto the second year. Although the second year was a bit more challenging I continued to excel. Not only did I pass with flying colours but I secured a 3 year apprenticeship with the UK's largest railway company as an Electrical Engineering Apprentice.

So in the space of two years I went from leaving school with poor grades to securing an apprenticeship with the UK's largest rail renewal and Maintenance Company. This was all down to perseverance and doing whatever it took. I always knew that I wanted to be successful and I was and still to this day always willing to work hard; very hard!

I started the apprenticeship in 2007, aged just 18, and passed when I was 21 in 2010. I could safely say this was a period where I went from a boy to a man. I moved out of my parents' house, bought my first car and in the last year I started working alongside grown adults, so I had to grow up fast. Paying bills, budgeting for food shopping and other expenses was tough at 20 years of age but it had to be done. At that time my rent was

£600 and as an apprentice I was earning just under one thousand pounds per month. Living like this made me even more determined to complete my apprenticeship and hit the "big bucks" so I could start living it up.

After a year or so of hard work I finally passed out of my apprenticeship. I signed my contract as a fully qualified engineer and all I could think about was moving up the ladder and getting promoted. A pattern formed because anything I focused on I achieved, and I was promoted to a senior position 6 months later. A few months later my company gave me the opportunity to go to university to take a foundation degree; this was all funded by the company and as I had aspirations of moving up the ladder this was a dream come true for me. It was just 6 years prior I was a failed schoolboy, my teachers said I wouldn't amount to much and there I was: handpicked to take an engineering degree as a fully qualified engineer. The course fees and expenses fully funded by the company, I was sure even back then that I was earning more than anybody in my year at school let alone my class and probably more than my teachers; I was extremely proud.

At age 21 I was earning around £50,000 per year; I worked extremely hard. It always seemed like there was never enough hours in the day and back then the only way I thought you would be able to make more money was by working more hours. I was working so many extra shifts at times; I would work 13 days straight, then one day off; another 13 days, one off and so on; it was crazy. My only break was when I had two week block release to go up to university where I slept through most of the lectures and seminars.

I remember sitting in the van with my colleague and friend, Chris, while we worked in central London and we would see cars like Ferraris, Aston Martins and Bentleys on a daily basis. I would always say "You know what? We will never be able to afford something like that working in this job." After all the years studying and working towards that dream job, I thought: is this what the real world is like? Sitting in a van in greasy overalls watching the wealthy enjoy life? I really didn't know what to do; at times I felt lost. I played the lottery quite often and I went to the casino with friends because I thought that rich people either inherited their wealth or got lucky by winning the lotto. It became more apparent to me that I needed to stop sitting on the sidelines.

I must admit, earning 50k at the age of 21 was above average and trust me I was grateful but I knew I hit the ceiling. By 22 I was earning 55k, by 23 I was earning around 60k a year and the funny thing was that the more I earned, the more I burned, and not only that, the tax man took a larger slice of the pie too! I thought to myself: I am 23, the glass ceiling is hit, there is no more earning potential, so by 33 I will be earning the same amount - a stagnant ten years! Remember at this time I was halfway through my foundation degree and barely passed; in fact, I stumbled across the line. My way of thinking and my attitude toward being just an employee had completely changed. Remember when I said I had dreams of moving up the corporate ladder and I was so proud of going to university to strengthen my chances of promotion? Well that plan was flipped completely on its head and I couldn't wait to finish university. To show you how glad I was to see the back of the place, I didn't even turn up to my graduation! My parents are still puzzled by this decision and they may even think that I failed to pass university but I can reassure them that I did. I'm just glad I didn't rack up any debt for that useless piece of paper... What a scam!

Now that the burden of exams and essays was out of the way I said to myself: "Enough is enough; it's time to start playing the game instead of watching from the stands" and that's when I started to think creatively and looked into entrepreneurship.

When I started my entrepreneurial journey I surfed the net and found some good information, and some bad information. So I decided to go to a seminar. After my first, I went to more seminars and one particular book kept being mentioned over and over again in all different areas of business and investing, whether it be stock trading, property, network marketing etc. The book was called *Rich Dad Poor Dad* by Robert Kiyosaki. I said to myself, "I need to read this book." I think I read it twice in under a week; every page just made me want to read the next. All I can say is that book changed my life; it changed everything: the way I looked at business; the difference between assets and liabilities; the way I viewed the education system.

At this time I had just one property but I quickly realised that I was running out of cash and wasn't able to leverage and/or raise funds so I had to be creative. I decided to go to a three-day property event. At this event I was blown away; I have never been to anything like it before so everything was new to me. Everybody in the room was full of so much energy, so talkative, so inspiring and, above all, everybody wanted to better themselves, not only as entrepreneurs but personally, which would then have an effect on their financial situation and future. As Jim Rohn said: "For things around you to change, first you have to change."

I met my business partner, Damian, at this particular event. The main reason I think we instantly had a mutual understanding, was because we were the youngest two people in the room - I think we were the only two people in the room under the age of 25, so that alone was enough to get us talking. We both signed up for the 12 month property mentorship programme and, fast forward three years, I now have a property portfolio that replaces my income. Was it easy? No! it was bloody hard! So many obstacles, so many times I doubted myself, so many times I wanted to give up, but was it all worth it? Yes it was, and the beautiful thing is, this is still just the beginning. I drive a supercar which I purchased at the age of 25 (I'm a petrol head). I will quote Jay Z on my journey so far, and this goes for me and all my business partners: "The genius thing we did was that we never gave up." Now I wish to share my knowledge and expertise - most of which has come from my head into this book. I hope you enjoy!

Introduction

Imagine waking up early 5 days a week for 40 years, fighting your way onto a sweaty tube for an uncomfortable 30-45 minute journey and finally reaching your destination – then being rewarded with doing a job you don't like for the next 7-10 hours. Doing just enough to stop you from getting fired, for a company paying you just enough to stop you from leaving. You get paid just enough to cover your bills, other expenses and some left over for your 2-week summer trip to Spain with the family, where you get a slight taste of freedom. Now picture fighting your way back home, drained after making your company owner richer than they already are, with just about enough time to scoff down dinner, spend an hour or so with your loved ones just before falling asleep in front of the TV.

Most people don't have to imagine this; sadly this is the reality for many. Ask yourself: is this the life I want to live for the next 40 years? 20 years? Or even the next 5 years? Really? Jobs and employment are no different from slavery or even imprisonment, just that the physical barriers have been swapped with financial barriers. Most people will totally get what I am trying to say here but for those who can't, simply ask yourself this one question: Am I free to do whatever I want; go wherever I want; with whomever I want – right this very second? If the answer is 'no' then you're a prisoner, my friend, just a well-paid one. The main problem is most people see this as just life: "Oh well, it's life I guess..." But we're here to show you there are ways to becoming financially free; there are ways to be able to do anything, anywhere, whenever you feel, with whomever you want.

Now imagine earning £3k a month and then earning another £3k passively from your business. What would you do? The choice is yours and that's the beautiful thing; you now have choices, which signifies control – control over your life, your future and the future of those you care about. We are here to show you that this can be your reality and life will improve if you commit yourself to learning and applying the skills required to change your circumstances ensuring financial freedom.

Whether you're 21 or 61, this can be achieved.

I remember one particular science lesson in school; the subject was biology. My teacher informed me that every cell in the human body regenerates itself every few years, meaning every few years, your body grows completely new hair, new skin cells, new liver, new stomach lining, new everything. This hit me like a ton of bricks around 5 years later. If the whole human body can regenerate then surely we must be able to reinvent our mind-set which will determine our level of success.

Jim Rohn once stated "Any two years you wish to drastically change from the previous two years, you can, but only if you really wish to." I am living proof of this along with my business partner, Damian. I went from using public transport in January 2014 to driving my dream car in July 2015: an Audi R8. You may be thinking that it's only a car, but if you met me in January 2014 and didn't see me again until July 2015, wouldn't you wonder what the heck I was doing? To be able to afford an Audi R8, there must have been a shift in my earnings – how did I achieve this? Damian went from delivering food shopping for a large company to being financially free, hence being able to leave his job and instead focus 100% on his business. Remember: a job is just a short-term solution to a long-term problem. Our lives have drastically changed since we first decided to invest in ourselves. So you're probably asking yourself, how did I get here; how did I end up in this position? How did I end up with a job paying me a salary that leaves me short of money at the end of the month and multiple streams of outgoings, i.e. bills and debt?

Trading time for money, and trading more time to play and make more money, is an inescapable loop which is self-fulfilling; you are essentially working for your first name and not for your last. People swap their time for money and then swap their hard-earned money for having a good time, i.e. drinking, holidays and acquiring liabilities. This is what I refer to as the self-fulfilling inescapable loop. Money in, money out, time traded for money, money traded for time-wasting.

The trick is to invest time and money at the start so you can reap rewards in the future. When I say "invest" not only do I mean business but I also refer to investing in your personal development so that you can educate yourself and ensure the best rate of return. Yes, education costs, but ignorance will cost you more in the long run. Yes, it's a risk, but the biggest risk is taking no risk at all.

The average person is 3 months away from being penniless if laid off from work for the same amount of time. The average person has debt of around £29,000 and has twice as much bad debt as they do savings. If you are in – or even close to – this category then you really, urgently need to take action NOW!

Chapter I

Mindset

Your mindset plays a very important part in your personal life, as well as in business. The education system is designed in a way that from a young age we go to school, study and move up the education ladder from primary school through to university in order to finally get a well-paid JOB.

Teachers tell us that we must pass our exams in order to progress further, which makes us scared of failure, causing stress. Then when we have graduated and start thinking about running our own business, we are still scared of failure so stay in our 9-5 JOB for a sense of security. Coming from Poland, where a similar – if not harder – education system is in place, I had several classmates who didn't progress to the next class for 2-3 years. I can only imagine how this affected their confidence; luckily I was not one of them. What is more concerning is that some of them may still lack confidence to this day!

T. Harv Eker says: "Rich people do what poor people only think about" – the difference between the rich and poor is that the rich are not scared of failure or losing money. They take a lot of action that turns into results and profits, whereas the poor only think or talk about their ideas, never taking action, which is why they are not succeeding.

Speed of implementation will determine how successful you will be: the more ideas you implement in your business the quicker you will gain success. If you don't pass your end-of-school exams, it doesn't limit your chances of success. There are a lot of very successful, high school and college drop-out entrepreneurs such as: Richard Branson, the founder of Virgin; Steve Jobs, co-founder of Apple; and George Foreman, the founder of the Foreman Grill.

Usually A grade students work for C grade students and B grade students work for the government.

From a young age, most of us are programmed with aspirations of going through the traditional education system (school, college, university), getting a well-paid job and buying a house, a car… The job will usually require a lot of hard work with the intentions of climbing the promotion ladder, whilst paying a pension for when we eventually retire after 40 years – at least.

When we are young we soak up information like a sponge, but if it's inadequate, it could be a waste of time – especially if it indirectly impacts on our future. As much as a third of university graduates are now working as cleaners, road sweepers or office assistants! Our society is changing again; similar to the industrial age, we will soon have to say goodbye to the service industry as we know it. You – we – are being replaced by machines and systems that require less employees, meaning jobs will be lost. This is already happening. The government pensions are not even secure anymore so what will you do if you retire to find the money you've been relying on isn't available? This is why it's very important to educate yourself and acquire assets such as property, stocks or building a business so you can control your life and secure your future.

In the information age, working 9am-5pm for somebody else will never make you rich, no matter how high you are in the company and how hard you work. The reason is that you will exchange your time for money and you will be building someone else's business instead of yours, and even if you earn good money you will not have time to spend it or enjoy it. You will not have time for your family either or, in some cases, after paying all of your bills, your car, mortgage and food you will be left with not much or nothing, and will have to live pay check to pay check. That is not what life is all about. You need to enjoy it, even if you receive a good income by working for somebody else, you usually get a bigger house, better cars and spend a lot of money on holidays which means that the expenses are much higher, and after the month ends there is not much left or the money is put on the side for holidays or something else. Instead, you should be saving money to acquire assets that will produce passive income without you physically working for it, so you can do things you love. If you don't invest, your income will always be related to your hourly worth. You will only make more money by working more and more. You need to remember that time is the only thing you can never get back. People spend money on luxuries and when the time for retirement comes they have to rely on government pensions that are very low, making it hard to survive. Especially when you get ill, you will have to forget about holidays and any luxuries. Retirement is the time that you deserve after working hard all your life for someone or by running your business, and you need to enjoy it, love it and go to see and discover different places. The only way you can achieve financial freedom is to invest, because savings are not good enough and pensions are dying.

When starting a new business, there is one important thing you need to remember. It happened to me (Damian) in my previous business where I failed many times. Never ever, ever give up! I was working on my new business venture I carried on for some time and when the tough times came I stopped because I thought this wouldn't work or maybe this is not the right type of business for me. It wasn't the business, but it was me that had to change. I kept jumping from one business to another expecting fast results within the first few months, and if things did not work out straight away I would give up and start something new. Before Thomas Edison invented a light bulb, he failed many times but he never gave up. He said, "I have not failed; I've just found 10,000 ways that won't work." Many of life's failures are people who did not realize how close they were to success when they gave up. Our greatest weakness lies in giving up. The most certain way to succeed is always to try just one more time.

We need to remember that there is something called the learning curve and also that success is not a straight line to the top with a golden path as some people think. There are times when you get good results; everything goes well at the beginning, and then finally problems arise and the business goes through tough times. It might happen many times but if you don't give up, but rather carry on and put a lot of effort into it, you will get back on track and you will be rewarded. This is how rich people are made. When the tough times come and problems arise they carry on and don't think about giving up. They will focus on the problem and start thinking of finding new ways, options and alternatives to solve it; they will ask themselves how they can improve it. Entrepreneurs are problem solvers; entrepreneurs are very creative and always find a way of fixing things and pushing through tough times, without jumping from one thing to another because something is not working. You need to master one field, and if you get good at it and become successful you can move to a new business venture. It takes roughly 10,000 hours to be an expert in a specific field. You can't graduate from university as a doctor and perform heart surgery the very next day. You need to practice, learn and experience first. The same happens in business. I never gave up on my property journey and that is why I succeeded.

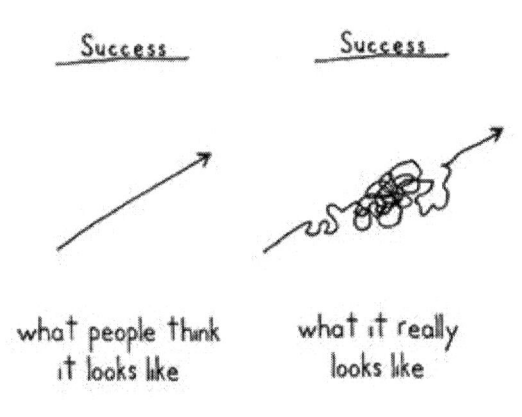

Success / *Success*

what people think it looks like / what it really looks like

If you feel as if you are stuck somewhere or don't know where you are going or how to improve personally or in business, we would highly recommend to get books that talk about mindsets that will help to unblock you. The three books we recommend are: *Awaken The Giant Within* by Anthony Robbins, *Secrets Of The Millionaire Mind* by T. Harv Eker and *Rich Dad Poor Dad* by Robert T. Kiyosaki.

If you want to be successful in life you should set goals firstly; you need to know where you are, where you want to be (what you want to achieve), how you are going to get there and when you are going to get there. In other words, it is a commitment to completion; make a commitment to yourself that you will follow any instructions and do whatever it takes to get where you want to be. Don't let people tell you can't do something; do not listen to anyone that tells you it can't be done. Keep going and never give up; stay positive and if you have a bad day, which you sometimes will (everyone does!), think about your why. Think about who you are doing this for; it will help you to get back on the right track (be focused). Only hang around with people who will encourage you and wish you the best and support you. You might lose some friends in the process – if they gave up on their dreams don't let them steal yours! Remember that who you hang around with is who you become. Try to surround yourself with people who want to achieve the same goals as you, are on the same mission, and with those that are already successful and have achieved what you want to achieve. In business, it is about who you know and who knows you. Your network = your net worth. Find your closest networking events where you can meet those types of people, sign up to more exclusive gyms, go to Angel investor's network in your local area, flying clubs, etc. We will talk about it more in the Raising Finance chapter.

Now: get out of your comfort zone and focus on what is important for you and on things that will bring you money and move you towards your goals – take action! You need to sacrifice and stop watching TV, stop spending hours on social media, stop going to the pub every weekend – this money could be invested into starting your own business and acquiring assets. Acquire wealth first so you can live the life that you deserve, spend time with whom you want to spend it, and go where you want to go without worrying about money. Many people use the excuse that they are "too busy;" however, there are usually several hours spare at the end of each day. If you break it down and record what you do each day and for how long, at the end of a week you will discover exactly how many more hours you have spare. You need to eliminate activities that cost you time and money. This is the same system that your personal trainer in the gym would use; if your goal was to lose weight, your personal trainer would tell you to note down everything you eat so they can measure your calorie intake and advise you of what foods to eliminate from your diet. Stop doing the things that don't get you results. All this time wasted will not build your assets, buy your dream car or give you financial freedom. You need to start making changes. Changes that will give you financial freedom and bring you closer to your goals. Figure out what these changes are for you and implement them immediately. If you do what you have always done you will get the same results as you always have.

Good Debt and Bad Debt and the Difference Between Assets and Liability

There are 2 different types of debt:

Good debt is when you take out a mortgage on a house you are going to let, as the tenant covers the mortgage and can give you an income. On the other hand, if you took out a mortgage and chose to live in the property you would be servicing the debt yourself, which would be a liability. We have many distressed owners calling us because they cannot keep up with their mortgage payments as a result of losing their job, getting divorced or any other personal reasons. In these cases, we off[er] them a solution. We will help them sell their house quickly, [in] some cases within 28 days time, and in exchange there will b[e a] discount on the property – it could be anything from 15-[40% or more] below market value, a win-win situation. The discount m[ay] depend on the conditions of the market – in the upmarke[t the] percentage will usually be less than the down market. Wh[en the] mass is buying, you should be selling, and when they are [selling] you should be buying; do the opposite and don't fol[low the] crowd. We need to remember that good deals won't com[e] easily – you need to find and negotiate for good deals.

Bad debt could be a car that you bought on finance and [have] to pay it off every single month for 4-5 years, taking m[oney] from your pocket. Don't get me wrong, there is nothing wrong with buying a car, but you should acquire some assets first that can pay for your car so you don't have to rely on a salary from a job to pay for it. Another example of bad debt could be a holiday that you bought on your credit card. People find themselves luxuries they cannot afford. If you get rich, you could be on holiday every single day and work from your laptop.

These days, technology is so advanced that all we need is an internet connection and we can operate our business from anywhere in the world. There is nothing wrong with using a credit card, but use it to your advantage; raise money when you don't need it so when the opportunity arises you are ready to grab it. We have funded many of our property investments through credit cards and loans. This is known as leverage; you can borrow money for deposits, renovations, etc. which is a clever use of credit cards, unlike a holiday you will be paying off for couple of years. We have also used our credit card to fund our education, which is another example of good debt; it is good to invest in yourself as you are your biggest asset. Going forward this helps you to minimise the risk of making mistakes. You could go and do it by yourself, you could still make it, but it will take you much longer and you will lose much more money along the way. From all the investments we have done, investing in ourselves was the best investment we have ever made. Please go to www.masterthepropertygame.com to watch our interview with George Ross–Donald Trump's right-hand man – to find out why the right education and coaching is important in business, and why property is one of the best assets to invest in. As mentioned previously your own home should also be classified as a liability. Those words come from real estate Guru Robert Kiyosaki, best known for writing the bestselling book *Rich Dad Poor Dad*. He changed the perception of people's thinking, and we agree that your home is not an asset. Even when you pay your mortgage off, you will still have to pay taxes and bills. The house you live in won't bring you an income each month; it will leave you with outgoings each month. This is classed as a liability. An asset is only something that puts money into your pocket. For example, watches, diamonds or art are assets as you only pay once and they increase in value. In one of our favourite books, *Rich Dad Poor Dad*, Robert Kiyosaki talks about the cash flow quadrant:

1. E- Employee – when you have a JOB (just over broke)
2. S- Self Employed – you own a job, if you are not there, you don't make money
3. B- Business Owner – you own a system and people work for you
4. I- Investor – money works for you

If you have a JOB or you are self-employed, you need to set goals, create an action plan and implement to move onto the B or I side of the quadrant where the big money is; the place where you can leverage your time and pay less tax. You can start part-time when you are still in a job and move on when you are ready. We all have 24 hours a day; it doesn't matter if you are Bill Gates, the cofounder of Microsoft, or Warren Buffet, the CEO and the largest shareholder of Berkshire Hathaway. The reason why they are amongst the richest men on the planet is simply because they don't exchange time for money, and they hire people to work for them. They leverage other people's time, effort and expertise to grow their business. This is how you get rich; if you had 100 employees working towards your vision and your business 8 hours a day, you now have 800 hours instead of just 24. Only do the things you are good at and love doing; delegate and outsource the rest. If you are on the right-hand side of the quadrant, you are the person that comes with a vision and a mission while you get other people to implement it.

"Wall Street is the only place that people ride to in a Rolls Royce to get advice from those who take the subway."- Warren Buffet.

If you want to move to the right-hand side of the quadrant where business owners and investors are, you need to start thinking BIG. If your dreams and aspirations don't scare you, you are not thinking big enough! You need to raise your standards. Each and every one of us has a financial thermostat, similar to the one we have in our homes. If you set it to 20 degrees, it will reach that temperature and stop. Then when it goes below that temperature the process will start again. The same happens in your mind; if you think that earning £100,000 makes you rich and that is the maximum you can earn, your financial thermostat and belief systems will be maximised and you will start spending as if you were rich. For some people, £100,000 could be a lot of money and for some people it's not – this is because of the standards they set for themselves. So what you have to do is set your financial thermostat for £1 million, £10 million or £100 million. How do you think Richard Branson would feel if he had £10 million in his bank account? He would feel broke as his financial thermostat is set to billions, not millions.

If you want success you need these three important ingredients:

1. Happiness
2. Health
3. Wealth

You cannot make it without all three. If you are not happy, you will not have the motivation to drive you to success. You need to know your reason why and be passionate about what you are doing. If you do not take care of your health through lack of exercise and eating junk foods, in time, this will have a negative impact on your performance.

Steve Jobs, the cofounder of Apple, would have paid billions to have his cancer treated. You could have all the money in the world but without your health it wouldn't mean much. That is why you need all 3 ingredients. There are situations sometimes that you can't control, but at least try to eat healthy food and exercise to reduce the risk of illness. Forget about the past and what you have learnt so far; if that didn't bring you any results, you cannot expect to do the same things and get different results. If you are broke, struggling and in a lot of debt, you need to focus on finding solutions. If you focus on the problems, guess what? You will attract more problems. If you want to be rich, you need focus on what you need to do to be rich and how to achieve it. In business you will face a lot of struggles and obstacles – that is just the way it is. There is no easy path, there is no elevator to success; you have to take the stairs. But if you don't give up and keep going, the rewards will be tremendous. Solutions and creativity are the keys to success. Every single entrepreneur needs to have the ability to solve problems. You need to think outside the box, be creative and look for different options; you need to be bigger than your problems.

Most millionaires and billionaires are self-made. They started from the same point where some of you are right now. It just goes to show that anything is possible and that anyone with the right mind-set and self-belief can achieve greatness. First of all you need to educate yourself; read books by the experts in your field, attend seminars/webinars and most importantly: take action! The best way to learn is by being active so you can learn from your mistakes and master the field of your interest. "To know and not to do is really not to know." Stephen R. Covey

You become what you are thinking about most of the time. When you are thinking, you create images in your mind. If you think about home, you create an image of your home. It is like a screen in your mind. If you think about work, you create an image of your work. The body is the instrument of the mind. How you think is how you act. When most people think about money, they visualise bills, their next pay cheque and debt. In order to eliminate these negative connotations, you need to reprogram your mind and the way you view money. Instead, think of your dreams, being financially free and being able to spend your time and money as you please. To help you change your mind-set, write your weekly, monthly, and yearly goals; create a vision board with pictures of anything that motivates you. To make this purposeful, you must read your goals and study your vision board every morning when you wake up and every night before you go to sleep.

This will also be your "why" when obstacles or bad days arise – it will motivate you and keep you going.

Most successful people use the law of attraction without even knowing it. To understand the law of attraction, we recommend you watch the movie or read the book called The Secret by Rhonda Byrne.

Chapter I I

Property: The Fundamentals

Property History

Property is one of the best models to invest in; not only is it a tangible asset, meaning you can see it and touch it, but over time property has always moved in an upward trend with regard to its value. Everything you see inside or from the outside of the property determines the value, i.e. the condition, size and number of rooms, the windows, floors, location and much more. The tangible aspect means an experienced or educated investor can make an informed decision with regards to its worth by simply viewing it.

The need for property will never ever go away. We all need a place to call home, so there will always be a demand for properties. Think about it; the United Kingdom is just a tiny island and there is a shortage of property. With the population growing at a rate faster than ever, this is great news for investors; too many people but not enough houses with a limited amount of space to build them on! In London, for example, developers are beginning to build downwards – that's right – there has been a new trend of basement apartments on the market.

Now, we're not saying that property doesn't come with ups and downs – it does. The housing market in the United Kingdom is cyclical just like any other market or business, but the long-term trend – as mentioned earlier – has always risen.

Just like any other market such as stocks and forex, there will always be external factors that influence property price trends, such as the economy and what's going on in the media. However, more common are factors that also have an effect on the market, such as supply and demand, interest rates and access to finance.

In property, the only constant is change; with change comes opportunity, and there are tons of investors that have taken advantage of the changes in the property world. Remember: if you are educated and have the right people around you, it's very hard to go wrong in property.

A lot of wealthy individuals – some well-known – that have initially acquired their wealth outside of property, have chosen to invest their money in property. Why? Because it's as the saying goes: it's as safe as houses. Property has created a vast amount of accidental landlords. It's very hard to lose money in property. Yes, you may have plenty of hardships in the short-term due to voids, bad tenants, inexperience and lack of knowledge but 10, 20, 30 years down the line, once rental prices and the value of property rise, your profit will outweigh those small losses by a huge margin.

There is a Chinese proverb that says 'the best time to plant a tree was 20 years ago, the second best time is now!' So don't wait to buy property; buy property and wait. As a prime example, I (Shane) bought a 2-bedroom property in South East London in February 2013 for £154,000. I recently got it valued in December 2015 and it is now worth £240,000 – a staggering £86,000 profit! Now what if I would have waited? Furthermore, what do you think is going to happen over the next 3 years or so? Yes, there may be one or two corrections in the market but overall the price will always be on the rise. Ideally you want to make money when you buy. This requires a lot more skill and finesse, which will be explained in a later chapter. Nevertheless, money will be made in the long run.

Unquestionably, there are times that are better to invest in property than others – having said that with a bit of experience and property education there are still opportunities during the bad times. For example, 2008 (a bit before my time as I was still in college), was named to be the worst correction in 20 years, just after the crisis with many large UK banks. Housing prices peaked massively, due to the banks approving mortgages to anyone that had a pulse, and then started a rapid decline, which in turn sent a lot of property investors bankrupt; on the other hand, the ones that positioned themselves correctly made millions, not just in the UK but worldwide.

A skilful investor is a pro at identifying opportunities while others are sceptical, not just in property but in any market. Remember: when somebody is losing money there is somebody out there making money – which would you prefer to be?

Like everything, property too has its risks but to reiterate: with the right education and thorough due diligence, the risks become very manageable. Did you know that property has a natural compensating mechanism? For example, a weakness in house prices is balanced out with a strength in rents – this is why you tend to have higher yields with properties outside of London than in London.

Let's expand on this: When housing prices crashed in 2008, this was due to tightened mortgage accessibility and crippled by the media; first time buyers refused to buy and opted to rent. Now, remember what I mentioned about supply and demand? With the majority of the UK wanting to rent, this then drives up rental prices. With repossessions of inexperienced landlords and first-time buyers happening left, right and centre (leaving them with adverse credit only allowing them to rent), this again reduced the amount of properties available to rent and in turn raised the demand for rental properties.

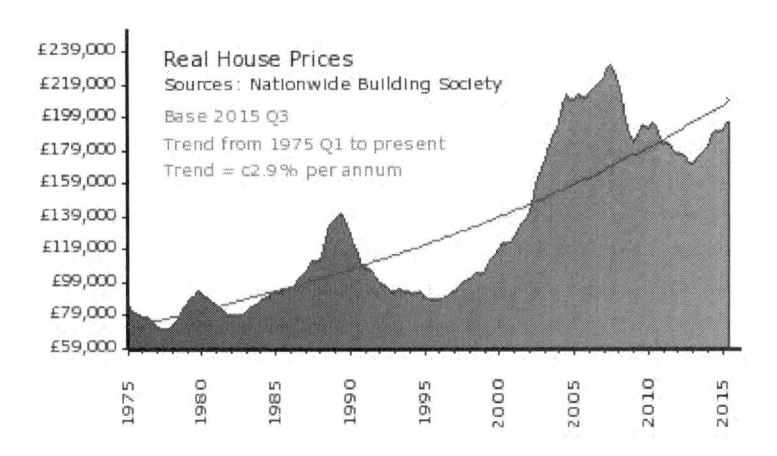

Real House Prices
Sources: Nationwide Building Society
Base 2015 Q3
Trend from 1975 Q1 to present
Trend = c2.9% per annum

The graph shown above displays the high points and the low points since 1975. The average rise according to www.housepricecrash.co.uk has been 2.9% per annum. The line indicates the average trend over the past 40 years.

You must have a love for property in order to benefit from it. You have to love what you do, so if property does not interest you in any way, shape or form, I recommend you find a different investment vehicle. Damian and I are property addicts. When I walk past estate agencies, I can't help but have a peer through the glass at the listings, just to see what the average prices are along with the local rental rates. I love picking up keys from an agent and taking the first look at my latest investment. I love the echoing sound of my shoes on the laminate flooring bouncing off the walls of an empty house which will soon be a home for a young professional, a group of students or a young family. I love property.

You need to have the same love and burning desire to succeed in property; it's all about YOU and your willingness to take time the time out to educate yourself with the skills needed to be successful in property investing. Not only do you have to take the time to educate yourself but also be willing to go out and put the skills you have acquired into practise.

You have to concentrate on your goals and take daily, consistent action – even if it's just an hour per day. It's all internal as nothing external matters. When you want something really badly, you should let nothing stand in your way. It's not going to be easy, but you should be willing to pay the price for your dreams and aspirations. Remember: anything that comes easy won't last, and longevity is credibility.

Due Diligence

Due diligence plays a very important part in property investing; I would say it is the most important aspect and it needs to be conducted correctly. It doesn't matter whether it's the buying stage, location, the right broker, finding the right agency, the right tenants, finding the right building contractors – even property education! The list is endless and due diligence should never be overlooked as a property investor.

Why is it so important? Sometimes the deal or lead you get from the potential seller might look great. They tell you the house is worth £100,000 and they are willing to accept a 20% discount for a quick sale, but when you check the real value it comes out that the property is only worth £80,000. We've been through this many times; what looked like a great deal turned out to be deceptive. There are many properties on the market for the same price so why would you bother with that deal when you can cherry pick any property that is on the open market for the same price? It would be a waste of time and money spent on marketing and branding.

Never, ever make assumptions. Making assumptions can make an ass out of you and me hence the word assume (ass u me). So Rule 1: Never make assumptions.

What I am about to explain is not just theoretical, as it is advice taken through our personal experience. Remember: to master the property game, you first have to be a disaster at the property game. Let me walk you through.

When you ask the vendor where they got the value of their house from they usually say things such as: "My neighbour told me…" or "The estate agent valued it." We call it a neighbour's valuation system: "My Neighbour Said." Quite often, estate agents have never valued the property; the seller just says that to make it sound credible. The closest they've got to a valuation tends to be phoning the local estate agency and asking how much the houses go for in the area. The typical reply from the agent will be in the bracket of £80-120K – never a fixed price as each property is different. They can't tell you how much a property is worth without seeing it. If they do go to value a property, they usually over price it; they do that for two reasons: 1) the more they sell it for, the bigger the commission they get and 2) to push the property market.

There are many tools available these days to get the actual value of the house. Professional investors use Home Track that is used by 95% of the Royal Institute of Chartered Surveyors (RICS); it's an expensive system but it gives very accurate values and can save you a lot of money in the long run. There are also several free tools available such as Zoopla or Right Move used in the

UK market where you can check sold prices and values of the properties. There is one simple thing that you need to remember: a property is worth as much as someone is willing to pay for it. So if somebody puts the house on the market for £100,000, it does not mean it's worth that much. This is likely to be a price that the owner would like to receive for their property. The asking price is often significantly higher than the realistic value of the property.

When we do our due diligence, the first thing we look at is sold prices on the same street and in the area of 0.25-0.5 mile. We find answers to questions for our own research; when was the last house sold in the area; how much did it go for; is it the same structure as the house that we are looking to buy (the same amount of bedrooms, bathrooms, WC, etc.). Sometimes if you dig really deep, you can find information such as when the property was first put on the market and how long it took to sell. This will give you a rough idea of the area's saleability.

What is the rental demand in the area? How much rent can the property achieve? What sort of tenants will the property attract? What's the unemployment rate in the area? What is the population? Is it in a good location? Is it close to a university or train station and, if so, could it be turned into HMO to generate a higher return simply by renting rooms individually? How much will it cost to turn it into an HMO? What type of license will you need? Different countries and councils have different regulations so you will need to check how that works in your local area.

These are all the questions you need to ask yourself before buying a property. Speak to at least five different estate agents in the local area and ask questions. If they are local, they know the area very well and they might be able to give you some golden nuggets that will determine if it is a good investment or not. This will also give you a rough idea of the property value. You must make sure you go and see the property before buying it, as looks can be deceiving and you may lose money as a result of making a hasty deal. There are horror stories about people buying property at an auction without seeing it first and after travelling 200 miles, they find the property is not there as it got burnt down 18 months ago.

While capital growth will be what you hope for over the longer term – and while history suggests you will get it – in the short term, most property investors focus on cash flow. In particular, make sure your mortgage repayments and other costs will be covered.

Most people believe their biggest asset is their home, but they're wrong. A property is only a true asset if it's servicing its own debt and producing an income. If you have a mortgage and use part of your salary to pay it every month, then the uncomfortable reality is that your home is probably your biggest liability.

Most landlords aiming to build portfolios for the purpose of providing an income tend not to use letting agents. However, to save on money is going to cost you in time as you end up doing all the donkey work until you have a big enough portfolio to employ someone part-time to help. That works out cheaper than an agency and this is the exact method we have used.

Insurance

Landlord insurance is a growing area, with an increasing number of specialist policies covering everything from standard buildings and content risks, to loss of rent, boilers, heating and other appliances.

Not having the right insurance can be very costly, as I (Shane) have discovered. I had a vacant property in Durham, in neighbourhood where copper theft is very common. The property was broken into, and all the pipe work was removed along with the boiler. Here's the worse part –as the water was left on, the property was flooded all the way through from the bathroom to the carpets, which damaged the joists, walls, paintwork, etc. I had insurance but in one of the clauses it stated that the insurance was only valid while the property was tenanted and not while it was vacant, so therefore I wasn't covered for the damage. I learnt the hard way for not being thorough with my due diligence; this cost me £9000.

What to Buy and What Not to Buy

There are some types of investments you should avoid; the first one is overseas investments. There are many people offering overseas property deals to investors. One of the reasons for this is the lack of interest from investors in their own country. These are usually overpriced, and combined with the lack of knowledge of overseas legislations (i.e. tax, law and economy), this could turn out to be one of the worst investment decisions made. Above all, if you do not know the country, do not speculate.

The second type of investments you should also avoid are off-plan and new builds. In some cases, a lot of money has been made investing in off-plan deals prior to the recession in 2008. An example of this would be 10 units purchased for £100,000 each and sold on completion for £150,000 each.£500,000 is a good return, but for those who failed to sell before the recession lost out as house prices dropped by 40-50%. To make things worse, many major banks stopped lending to developers so many projects were left incomplete. Investors lost out big time! Again, this is a prime example of making sure you are in control of your investments and assets.

New Builds

We were working on a deal that came through our website – it was a 3-bedroom flat in a tower block in Liverpool. It was a lovely flat with a concierge on the ground floor, 5 minutes drive from the town centre with excellent transport links. We did all our due diligence and we managed to negotiate a 25% discount on the property. The final step was to send the RICS surveyor to value the flat – the seller bought it for £69,000 in December 2011. We knew that the flat did not go up in value and it was worth roughly the same in 2014. So with a discount of 25%, we negotiated a price of £51,750. When the valuation of the flat came back, we were both shocked and couldn't believe it. The value of the flat was less than £40,000. The reason the flat had devalued was because a newer block of flats, that had been built nearby, failed to sell, causing all property prices in the area to be reduced and new builds were hit the hardest.

Why would someone pay more money for the exact same property next door?

This is how you can lose money in new builds, so we backed out of the deal. Although we put some time into due diligence for this property and paid for a surveyor, it was worth the £500 to ensure we didn't go into the deal blindly, potentially losing £1000s. Remember, you can only do so much due diligence yourself, so always invest in a surveyor.

Systems

The main reason for building a property portfolio is to give us freedom. This will allow us to travel the world, build other businesses and spend as much time as we want with our loved ones. You need to work on the business rather than in the business! You don't want to be an investor having to do all the work yourself.

When we started investing in our first properties, we wanted to be involved in the day-to-day issues: Fixing doors, toilets, locks, leaks, you name it. Most of the properties we started with were HMO's in London with at least 5-6 rooms with one tenant occupying each. There was a high turnover of tenants.

We also did the viewings, move ins and outs which was time consuming. Even more so when rooms were left in poor condition and required new furniture or a fresh coat of paint etc. We did all the painting and decorating by ourselves, we went to buy new furniture we even had to transport it and assemble it ourselves. This demanded a lot of our time and energy and instead of searching for new properties and deals we were doing the £10 jobs that could be done by somebody else more skilled than we were. In that time lost, we could have concentrated on what's important: deals! Acquiring assets that bring us thousands of pounds. In the beginning through lack of understanding we worked hard not smart. We managed tenants directly from our mobile phones, they would call us at any time with all kinds of issues. This had a negative effect on us and would often effect our moods, at times it drove us crazy and we knew something had to change.

We would run around day by day doing viewings, sometimes we would travel to the other side of London, wait in traffic for 3 hours to find that the people coming to view had cancelled last minute.

You need to know what steps to take to overcome these sort of issues. You can emulate the step-by-step formula taught at our seminar and throughout our coaching programme. Everything taught is based on our trials and tribulations over the past few years in running our property business. Visit our website to find out more information about our upcoming live events and coaching programs at www.masterthepropertygame.com.

In order to free yourself from day-to-day issues that arise, you need to systemise. Bring in staff to deal with tenant issues and administration; bring in somebody to conduct viewings and manage your property portfolio. Or simply just one person full time to carry out all of the above. Doing this will allow you to run your property empire from anywhere in the world as long as you have internet access and your power team. In this day and age you can outsource admin work etc to India and the Philippines. This allows you to keep costs down and focus on expanding your property portfolio; you can find employees that will do all those jobs for very little money so you can focus on adding more and more properties that will bring serious money to your pocket.

Prior to systemising, it's important to document your daily activities when running your property business. This could be from the way you conduct viewings, structuring adverts to writing contracts etc. When you look to bring in staff and streamline your business you have to remember that you are the most experienced person; everything you know has to be easily duplicated. There are 2 ways to do this: You can voice record your actions using various recording apps or you can simply note them down by hand or via word document. Its best to type out using bullet points so everything is clear and simple to follow. Once the business is systemised and running on its own, you can move on to your next business venture, systemise again and start a new business venture again and again.

This is how the richest entrepreneurs make their money – they leverage their time and this is why they achieve so much so quickly. They have vision and let others help make their vision a reality. The quicker you systemise the better. If the business is not systemised as in the business doesn't work, if the business depends on you then it's not a real business – it's not saleable, viable or valuable.

Own your property portfolio and life, don't let it become another full time JOB, don't let it own you. As business owners we ask ourselves questions and come up with many excuses: "I can't systemise the business, I don't trust people, I am the best at doing the job", No you are not! , I can't employ people, I don't have money to pay people" Trust me, there is always a way of making it work – you just need to think outside the box and you can have it all.

Mistakes and Golden Rules When Investing in Property

Only deal with **motivated sellers directly**. What do I mean by this? All the best deals are out there but not at the estate agents. There are people still buying and finding deals with estate agents but it's much harder as you can negotiate on the price but not on the terms.

Estate Agents do their own marketing to attract potential sellers. They send leaflets out in the local area or market through newspaper ads; this is how they find most of their deals.

Why can't you just skip the middle man and go directly to the seller? Start doing your own marketing, this can be done even if you are still in a full-time job, get leaflets printed and post them through letterboxes before or after work or hire somebody to deliver it for you.

When you get a phone call from a vendor, you need to ask him specific questions to find out how motivated they really are; you need to ask why they are selling or how fast they need to sell? This will give you some idea on how motivated they really are, if they are not in a rush and it's about the price and urgency, they are time wasters and not the kind of people you want to deal with as they are not motivated sellers. You just need to move on to the next one – property is a **numbers game** and from 100 leads, you might purchase 1-3 properties. Is it worth it? Absolutely! If you make roughly £40,000 per month every other month, it's definitely worth the time and couple of hundreds of pounds invested on marketing. Some people get paid a £40.000 per year salary working for someone hard, 9-5, 5-6 days a week. You can make that in a month by spending a few hours on the phone working from home or on your laptop anywhere in the world.

Put as **little money down** into the deal as possible – the less money you put down, the higher the return on investment. You can buy houses without using any of your own money, too. We will show you how in the next chapters.

Cash Flow is King – most of the time when investors buy properties, they think about capital appreciation, meaning that an increase in the price or value of the property is where the investor will make their money. We agree that over time historically property has always increased in value, but we can't predict the future and what will happen in the next 10, 20, 30 years in the property market. We treat property capital appreciation more like a bonus.

You need to make sure that there is a sufficient amount of positive cash flow every month from each property. Never, ever buy property that will break even or will take money away from your pocket every month, as the property will therefore become a liability rather than an asset and do not speculate or rely on the house's value growth! If you find a deal without any cash flow, let it go and unless there is a way of adding value to the property that can increase the rent to boost cash flow forget about it and move on. If it's in a good location, adding an extra room or adding a loft conversion can add value. But again, you need to look at the ROI; will the cost of adding value stack up? Remember as a rule of thumb, £200 from each property per month with 10 properties you are looking at £2,000 per month passively. It may seem like 10 houses is a lot but you can achieve this – in some cases within a year. We just gave a minimum figure of £200 that can be achieved with single lets. We have multi lets that bring us £900 per month. If you can acquire two of these you will be able to fire your boss. It becomes very easy once you have the knowledge and skills – success brings more success and results bring profits.

When you buy a house, always look at **today's value** of the property. Don't speculate on how much it will be worth in the future; always aim to make money instantly when you buy, not when you sell. Simply put; if you get a discount of 15-25% on a property purchase because somebody had problems and wanted to sell fast or was moving overseas, you make money straight away! If you are not into buying to hold and like to make fast chunks of cash, put it up for sale on the open market.

Protect your interest – Once the deal is negotiated with the vendor, make sure you sign documents that will give you exclusivity to complete the deal. The last thing you want is the deal to be swiped from under your nose after all the time, effort and money spent on due diligence.

Small is beautiful – When starting out in property investing, start small, with small houses or flats; don't get involved in big commercial buildings, large refurbishments and deals that you have no idea about. Once you gain the knowledge, experience and you master the property game, you can then step up to get office, conversions and large developments.

Keep your eye on the ball – Even if your business is systemised and running on its own, you have employees that are building your property empire and you are relaxing in Miami drinking a piña colada, make sure you are aware of what is happening in the company. Always check and measure; it's helpful to have one trusted employee to report to you. One that will keep you updated on the company's progress and financial condition. Trust but verify!

Chapter III

Raising Finance

There are many ways of investing in property, even if you don't have any money. Lease options and Rent to Rent are two very popular strategies. You can create a lot of cash flow by packaging and sourcing deals for other investors for a fee. However, it doesn't mean that if you don't have money, you can't invest in multi-million pound projects such as developments, commercial conversions or normal BTL properties worth a lot of money.

There are people out there who are waiting with their cash to invest in your deals instead of having their money in their bank where they're unlikely to get much return. Money loses value every single day and after paying taxes, they may just break even or make a loss. That is why they look for new opportunities. Some of those people are cash rich and time poor, meaning they don't have the time to find deals. These investors are looking for people like you to find and negotiate deals so they can finance it and share a profit with you. You need to start hanging around with these sorts of people; tell them what you do and build a relationship with them at the networking events, exchange business cards and after the event follow up with everyone the next day via email. You can say things like: "Hi Mr Smith, it was a pleasure to meet you at the property networking event yesterday. It would be great to meet up with you to discuss further business opportunities. Please let me know when you'd be free to meet up." Or you can say things like "There is no free lunch, but there is when I am in town." It all depends on who you deal with. This is just a simple example. If you are good at writing emails you can develop it, but try to keep it short and to the point. Remember: dress to impress; you can never get a second chance at a first impression. Who you hang around with is who you become and your network is your net worth. If you told us how much five of your friends made annually we could predict your salary.

We will name a few places and products where you can raise money for your property investments. Even if you have a lot of money and you start investing, you will eventually run out of money one day. That is why it's very important to raise finances and use other people's money instead of your own. All successful people do the same – they don't use their own money.

Joint Venture (JV)

This is a very good way of building your property portfolio quickly with minimal risk and no capital required. JV partners could be people who you meet at networking events. Some have a lot of time and will bring you good deals, whereas others are very busy but have a lot of cash to invest. If you are working with private investors they will have business experience that can help you. This will be very beneficial when analysing deals, legal issues, profit and loss etc. It is much easier and quicker to build a property business with partners than by yourself. Before entering in any JV agreement, make sure you do your due diligence on the person you are dealing with and consult with your solicitor. JVing with other people has positives and negatives so you need to analyse it before you enter such an agreement.

For a joint venture to work, you need to choose the right partners; each partner needs to bring something different to the partnership. It's important to have clear documents that outline how the partnership will work so you know who is responsible for what. You need to be honest and open with each other.

I (Damian) experienced bad partnerships many times and lost a lot of money in business but it wasn't their fault – it was mine. You need to take responsibility for yourself. If I had done enough due diligence on the people I was partnering with I would never have gone ahead with the deal. But I am happy that it happened as it was a good lesson and I will never make the same mistake again. It takes time to find good partners and you might be lucky and find a good one in the first place. Remember there is a golden rule in business: trust but verify! I have done many good deals with my current business partners and it would never have happened if I didn't go to networking events. Shane and I travelled all the way from London to Florida just to network and meet new people who we can do business with. That is called sacrifice; we do whatever it takes. Do today what others don't, to have a tomorrow that others won't.

You can also JV with your friends and family; you provide the deal and knowledge whilst they bring the money required. Once the work is done, you share the profit 50/50. There are many different ways of structuring JV deals. For example, there might be people who are not interested in monthly income but investing money for capital appreciation. So instead of sharing the profit 50/50, you take the cash flow every month and they take the equity. The amount the house appreciates in value will benefit your JV partner, but make sure you have an exit strategy in place so you don't have situations where they want to sell the property but you want to keep it.

Remember that 50% of the deal financed by a JV partner is better than 100% of nothing.

Crowd Funding

Crowd funding is getting more and more popular. There are a lot people with a good business plan and models but with limited finances. Raising money from banks is difficult and bridging is expensive. Many investors look for opportunities where they invest their money for a share in a company or project in return. It is very common in this day and age to start big developing projects where there are few investors that fund the project together to build apartments, and once it is sold they share a profit equivalent to the proportion of the money invested. In some crowd funding projects, anyone can invest money and get, for example, a 10% return on their investment. Quite often there are hundreds of people investing in one project. This is an extremely powerful strategy and it's now even used to raise money for start-up businesses and movies.

Credit Cards, Loans and Overdrafts

When we started our property journey we had no money and a lot of debt. Our favourite source of investment at the time was credit cards and overdrafts as we didn't know many people who we could raise the money from. Most of our credit cards were maxed out, so we had to increase our credit limits. Our first property investments came from none of our own money! When you have no money you must start thinking outside the box as you have little choice. These tips came from our mentors, they showed us how to do it and what to say when talking to the banks as this is very important. If you tell your bank that you need money to invest in property then you can forget about them agreeing.

From being broke, we both achieved financial freedom in just one year of investing in property. It all came from knowledge that we acquired from our mentors, books and creativity, so we managed to crush the myth that you need money in order to make money! If you want to master the property game, you need to have the knowledge to be creative. That is how winning is done. Most of the multi-millionaires and billionaires are self-made; they started from zero or debt, so anything is possible. You just have to believe it, set up a plan on what you want to achieve and how you are going to get there; for your dreams to come true you first have to wake up! You can have anything you want in life, you just have to be hungry and believe that you can have it.

Sylvester Stallone (Rocky Balboa) is a great example of a self-made millionaire. He started from humble beginnings – he was evicted from his apartment and was homeless for a while. In

March 1975 Stallone saw Muhammad Ali fighting against Chuck Wepner. After that fight, he went home and started writing a script, taking inspiration from both the fight and the autobiography of Rocky Graziano to start writing Rocky Balboa. Stallone attempted to sell his script to multiple studios with the intention of playing the main role in the movie. Although receiving enormous amounts of rejections, which went on for several months, he never gave up. He was finally offered $350,000 just for the rights to the script without him playing in the movie. He refused to sell it unless he could play the main character, so after a substantial budget cut to compromise the producers agreed to have him as a star, and the rest is history. He could have just taken the $350,000 which for him at that time was a lot of money, but if he did he wouldn't be where he is today. That shows determination. There was a time in his life where he had to sell his dog for $50 because he didn't have any money to feed him; after his success with the Rocky Balboa script, he bought his dog back for $15,000.

Angel Investors

There are a lot of places to go where angel investors spend their time. All you need to do is search on the internet for the closest one to your area. Millionaires and billionaires come to these places and look for people with great ideas for a new business where they can invest their money for a share in the company in return. More importantly, not only will they invest, but they will also give you all the support you need, which is priceless. They usually have their own power team that has expert knowledge in marketing, branding and selling. Of course, you must know everything about the business and have a great pitch that will attract the investors to persuade them to invest in your company or project.

You need to make sure you know your numbers; know everything about your competition, if there is any, and have a great unique selling proposition (USP). Having a mentor that has already achieved what you want to achieve is precious! I (Damian) have invested and started many companies before property investing. I invested all the money I saved from my part-time jobs and I lost it as well as getting myself into debt. The main reason I failed in both businesses was because I didn't know what I was doing. I had no guidance or a mentor to tell me how it needs to be done, what needs to be changed and what it is I was doing wrong.

When I started property investing, I had a mentor from the beginning and that is why I succeeded and I have done it in a very short space of time. I knew exactly where I was going and I knew that I had the support if I needed it. Every successful person has a mentor; imagine a footballer in the English Premier League or an athlete without a coach. Do you think Usain Bolt, the fastest runner on the earth, would be where he is today without a coach? We have paid a lot of money for mentoring and coaching, but with angel investors you can receive investments and free mentoring for a share in your business.

Family and Friends

There are a lot of people such as friends and family that have money sitting in their bank accounts without getting much return on their savings. Believe it or not, but money goes down in value all the time; inflation kicks in and prices go up. What you could buy for £10 ten years ago you can't buy anymore. That is why it's very important to invest in assets that appreciate in value. If you get a good deal, you can ask your friends if they would like to get 10 % return on investment on their money. I am sure they will like the idea as in the bank it's unlikely they'll get more than 1%. How you give it back is flexible; once the property is refinanced or pay them interest each month. It all depends on the individual and your agreement. Once they get their money back after the first deal, this will prove you can be trusted and they are likely to lend you money again.

Sell Liabilities

What do we really mean by selling liabilities? A liability is something that takes money out of your pocket, e.g. if you have a car that is worth £10,000, it will go down in value every single year plus it will cost you money every single month. Car insurance needs to be paid, road tax, petrol, MOT test, car maintenance and repairs. If you sell the car for £10,000 and buy a property below market value, you can refinance the property after 6 months and buy a new car or you can get a new car on finance as you will have a passive income from the house you bought. Every single month the rental income will pay for your car without you physically working to pay for it, so instead of having just a car, now you have a property plus a car that is paid by the asset you have acquired. What would you prefer?

Bridging Loan

A bridging loan is a very good method if you need to borrow money for a property that you want to buy very quickly. It only takes a few days for the bridgers to accept your application and lend you the money; in some cases 24-48 hours. If you borrow for the first time and pay back successfully the next one will be much easier and quicker because they know that you are reliable.

Bridging loans are mainly used by investors buying houses at auctions where you have to complete the purchase almost immediately. You cannot do the same with a standard mortgage company. Bridging loans have very high interest, from 1-3% per month or more in some cases. You need to know your numbers and have an exit strategy in place as it's a very risky loan. If you have never taken out a bridging loan, make sure you consult with a financial advisor beforehand or somebody that has experience in bridging so they can make you aware of the potential problems that can arise.

Social Media Groups

There are a lot of property investing groups on social media that you can join for free. You can ask questions, gain free advice and find potential business partners. You can even sell and buy property deals, subject to how active you are in the forums.

Before buying anything, make sure you do your due diligence on the person that is offering the deal and on the property they are offering. We had many deals that came our way but when we did our due diligence we found out that many of these properties were on Rightmove and Gumtree, revealing that we were not being offered a discount or, in some cases, they were trying to charge us above market value!

Seminars and Networking Events

This is our favourite way of raising finance, as most of the deals we have done and money we've raised came from people we met at seminars and networking events. Some people we know say that we are lucky because we manage to sell a deal or get a deal financed that made us a lot of money. But guess what? If we were sitting at home watching TV, playing PlayStation or going to the pub with friends, we would never have met the sources and our business partners. It's all down to our hard work and the time we spent building relationships and our network. Your network is your net worth. It's been mentioned a lot in this book but it's true; it's not who you know but who knows you.

You first need to invest some money into the relationship before you start to do business with anyone. We invite potential business partners for dinner, for example. Is food free? No, it isn't! Is transport free? No, it isn't! You need to pay for eating quality food, for petrol or a train ticket. People who say you are lucky forget about all the sacrifices, costs and hard work. Business relationships are similar to dating. You shouldn't ask for sex on the first date; it's the same in business. You need to meet multiple times and build a relationship with a potential business partner before you do any business together.

Private Members Club

There are many different types of private members' clubs. If you are a fan of cars, you could look into a Ferrari or Lamborghini private members' club. You don't necessarily need to own one to be a member. People who can afford these kinds of cars are definitely the ones with money so it could be a huge benefit to hang around with them and build relationships that could add value to your business in the future.

There are also yacht clubs, gentleman's clubs, luxurious concierge services where you pay a monthly fee of anything between £50-£200. You get access to the best clubs in your city for free where you don't need to wait in a queue. Impressive restaurants and sold out VIP events from the world of music to theatre, film, sport and art. There are many different private members' clubs to choose from – it all depends on what you are looking for and what interests you. You can find more information about private members' clubs online.

High End Gyms

The gym is a perfect place to network with people. There are reasons for that. First of all, you will see the same people every single day or at least 3-4 times a week because if you want to keep healthy and fit you need to work out on a regular basis. When you meet someone every single day and you make eye contact with them they will remember your face, and eventually you will start talking to each other. You will share weights, benches and equipment together and if they like you, you might even come to the gym with them at the same time and work out together.

The main reason that we mentioned high end gyms and not just any gym is because this is where wealthy people go to exercise. Wealthy people won't go to any local gym as they like luxury and great customer service – everything they need is in one place from nutritional guidance, private medical care, spa treatments to DNA testing to determine what exercise suits them best. They also want to hang around with other people who are successful because who you hang around is who you become.

High end gyms have very expensive joining fees, which could be anything from £400-600 and a monthly fee of around £185-240. The most expensive one in London is in Knightsbridge, which costs as much as £2000 to join and £500 per month. There are a lot of gyms to choose from that are also very good and attract successful people and cost much less. David Lloyds or Virgin Active gym will cost you around £70-90 per month. High End gyms cost a lot but sometimes it is money well spent. If you can find someone that could finance your project of £500,000 to £1,000,000 or JV with you, isn't the £200 per month worth it? Some people spend £3 on a coffee every single day, £3 x 5 days= £15 per week! In one month, that's a cost of £60. What if you could save this money instead and put it towards the gym membership that will be much more beneficial and healthier than your daily coffee?

There are many more places where rich people spend their time. A charity ball is a good place to go as people spend a lot of money there bidding and raising funds to help the less fortunate.

There are very cheap and also very expensive ways of raising money. Everyone's situation is different. You might be able to pay the £200 for the gym membership or you might prefer to go to free seminars or networking events. If you keep working hard and you are out often meeting new people, you will build your network and you will find the people who you are looking for. It might take you slightly longer than the more costly route as it may attract wealthier people, but you will still make it as you might meet someone who knows somebody who has the money and would like to invest it or get a better return than the bank is giving. We had to choose the cheap route as we were in debt so didn't have the money to join expensive clubs. We are a living example that you can build a big network without spending £200 per month on gym membership. We met most of our business partners and investors at networking events and seminars, but we worked really hard to build those relationships.

Chapter IV

How to Find Property Bargains

Different Types of Advertisement

We already know that the best place to find the best property deals is going directly to the vendor, so we can skip the middle man (agency) and negotiate not only on price but on the terms. If you buy through an estate agency, there is no chance to negotiate on the terms. In order for you to get access to the best deals, not only do you need to market the same way estate agents do, but you need to go above and beyond.

Place adverts in a newspaper on a regular basis; sometimes an add needs to be seen 4-5 times for a vendor to act on it. If you appear more often, the chances are higher that you will convince the seller to pick up the phone and call you. Make sure your message is appealing and it grabs the attention of the person reading it.

Leafleting can be a very good form of advertising and in our opinion converts the most, but instead of delivering 1000s of leaflets in different areas, circle one small area on a map and carry out repeat deliveries in the same area. Again, people will tend to take action and are more likely to grab the phone when they see your leaflet a few times. You need to create visibility and build trust. Bandit signs are another useful form of marketing, even though it can be risky. You can place them by the traffic lights or on a roundabout or any other place where there is a lot of traffic. You could also build a good relationship with grocery shops and leave your leaflets there or put a poster on the window. Speak to window cleaners that are known in the area and ask them if you could place small advertisements on their van for a monthly fee.

Lastly, we have the more expensive marketing techniques such as radio ads, Google AdWords and Facebook marketing. These techniques reach the masses and can be highly effective. If you can afford it, go for it! But if you are just starting out, with a small network, stick to the basics for now.

Split Testing

In marketing it's all about split testing. You need to run an advert for some time to see which ad performs best. Sometimes if you just tweak one word, it might convert 15-20% more. You need to try different words, different phrases, different fonts and colours of the words, numbers and backgrounds etc. If you don't test different things you won't know what works and what doesn't. There is no point of wasting money on an advert that doesn't work. We are very lucky these days as we can run a simple test through Google AdWords or Facebook where you put a budget of, let's say, £10 per day to see which advert performs better.

Numbers Game and Motivated Sellers Only

You need to remember that once you start advertising, you may receive 100s of calls per month. When we started our property journey, we were so desperate to seal our first deal that we put so much time and effort into every single lead that came our way.

We did our due diligence prior, then we called the seller just to find out that it wasn't about the terms and time. It was all about the price for the vendor and they wouldn't consider any kind of a discount. Our time was totally wasted, searching for things that didn't matter because the seller didn't want to sell their home for less than the market value. If the seller isn't motivated at all and it's all about the price for them, don't waste your time! Move on and begin searching for the next deal, as there will be many more. There is always someone that needs to sell their house quickly, for various reasons such as divorce, repossession, illness etc. Don't take advantage of them and make sure it's a win-win situation so all parties are happy. If you focus on offering them a quick solution that can help them to move on with their life in exchange for a small discount, this leaves everyone happy and the job done.

As stated previously, out of 100 leads maybe 20 will be interested in selling their house to you, and from that 20 you may end up buying 1-3 houses. The more leads you get through every month, the more deals you will close. If you can't buy all of them, choose the one that best suits you, package the remaining deals and sell them on to other investors for a fee. The money you get from sourcing will give you money for more marketing.

Chapter V

Cash Flow/Passive Income

What is Passive Income?

Income streams that come from sources that are received on a periodic basis, often with little effort to maintain. Passive income can include things such as rental income, royalties, dividends or pensions. The whole purpose of setting up a business and then systemising it is to become financially free so whether you are asleep or on holiday, you still get paid.

Money works for you instead of you working for money, you no longer have to exchange your precious time for cash. You work on the business not in the business. Passive income requires virtually no work, if you lay foundations and systemise correctly.

What is Cash Flow?

Cash flow is the amount of excess cash left over after all expenses have been paid. We have a positive cash flow if the gross income, i.e. rent, is more than all expenses but if not, it's called negative cash flow. See the example for a 3-bedroom house below:

Outgoings	Income
Interest only mortgage: £400	Rental income: £700
House insurance: £20	
Estate Agency managing fee: 10% = £70	
Maintenance: £25	
400+20+70+25= £515	Cash Flow = £700 - £515 = £185

Case study 1 - Buy to Let

Whitehorse Lane, London
Purchased May 2013
Property Type: 2 bedroom flat in converted house
Leasehold: 999 Years
Purchase price: £154,000
Market Value: £176,000
Mortgage interest only: £335
Rent: £1100
Ground rent and service charge: £186 per month
Cash flow: £579
Current value: £240,000

Different Passive Income Vehicles

There are many different vehicles and ways of creating passive income; one of the best ways to make passive income is through property. Once the house is rented and tenants fully managed, there is not much you have to do. Just wait for the money to come to your bank account every single month.

You can get dividends and interest income from owning securities, such as stocks and bonds. Another great passive income stream is forex trading. It's one of our favourite ways of making money. For those that don't know what forex is, it's a 24-hour market, where you buy and sell currencies; you can make money both ways whether the market goes up or down. Some mornings after waking up we find out that we have made hundreds of pounds from trades that we placed the night before. It's a great feeling not having to physically work for money and it comes so easily compared to the days where I (Damian) had to work really hard to make a few hundred pounds. I still remember the day when I failed in my first business and I lost all the money and I had to work night shifts in a shopping centre cleaning glasses to pay off my credit card debt, or the days when everyone enjoyed Sunday with the family and I had to go to work for £7.80 per hour, starting sometimes at 3/4pm and delivering groceries until 11pm. I felt really bad about it and I hated my job, but the main reason that I was doing it was to make some extra money to pay bills while I was building my property portfolio part-time. Sometimes you have to stay in a part-time job to make some extra money while you build your new business – there is nothing wrong with that and I would highly recommend doing it in such a way as it's easier. If you feel that you can start a new business without having a job on the side, go for it! But if I were you, I would make enough money first to make sure I can pay my bills.

You can also invest in commodities such as gold, silver, cooper, oil, gas and much more. There are many ways of creating passive income: ATM machines, coffee machines, royalties from publishing a book or from licensing a patent or computer software program, designing apps for mobile phones. If you are a good singer you can record and upload your songs on iTunes; you can make passive income from CDs, DVDs, online memberships, internet advertisements on websites, a laundry business, articles, slot machines, banner advertising, network marketing and much more.

Before you start investing in anything that we have mentioned, please seek legal as well as financial advice from a competent advisor before making any commitments. We share this information with you as a guide only and it cannot be considered as financial advice in any way. We just share our experience, our opinions and what works for us.

Why is it Important to Have Multiple Streams of Income?

Have you ever noticed that all the richest people in the world have more than one business?

The average millionaire has 7 income streams. There are many reasons for this; as the saying goes "Don't put all your eggs in one basket." Rich people think a few steps ahead, and have an entire strategic game plan. If there are loses in one business, they have several other income streams to balance the books while they come up with solutions. When businesses underperform, the average entrepreneur would look to lay off staff and cut back on things like marketing. A high turnover of staff and becoming invisible in the market place can destroy your brand and eventually your business. You should never, ever compromise on marketing and branding costs! This is the most important factor to keep your company alive and in the game. Cut everything else but don't cut marketing and branding costs.

McDonald's, one of the biggest franchises in the world, isn't about selling burgers as much as the real estate. The owner of the biggest fast food chain attributed most of the company's success to Harry Sonneborn, who worked for McDonald's for 10 years and whose real estate policies helped the company achieve great success. In the beginning Ray Kroc struggled to make the business profitable; the business did not generate enough revenue from the franchised restaurants. The main struggle for Kroc was raising money to pay for land and to fund the building for the restaurants. He had to franchise one restaurant at a time rather than a few stores over a particular geographic zone. The franchisees Kroc attracted didn't have the sort of money to pay for the land and building, unlike other fast food chains that were able to attract big investors.

Everything changed when in 1956 Kroc hired Sonneborn, who convinced the owner that the real money was in the real estate, not in the burgers. In the beginning, he came up with an idea to lease the building and the land and then sublease to the franchisees that would run the restaurants, Then Sonneborn came up with a new idea to own the buildings and lands via mortgages. McDonalds started off charging their franchisees markups of 20% of lease costs then increasing to 40%. As a franchisee you were responsible to pay for insurance and taxes, ensuring steady profits for the company as long as the restaurant remained in business. If the restaurant was performing very well, the franchisee had to pay either the lease markup or 5% of the sales, whichever was higher.

As a franchise, you also had to pay an up-front security deposit. These days, McDonalds is struggling and they will have to adapt more to the market, as people want to eat healthy food instead of fast food. But even if something goes wrong, they can sell the company's own multi-billion dollar real estate portfolio.

Our main business is real estate; this is where most of the money is made. We don't just rely on our real estate business; we are involved in many different business ventures and activities. Remember just in case something happens to one business, we have multiple streams of income to soften the blow. You can have multiple streams of property income; you can buy property to hold and rent; you can buy and sell; you can negotiate and package deals for other investors; or you simply sell leads to investors. There are many different ways of making money in property, and you don't need tens of thousands of pounds to start. You can make money without having any money. All you need is knowledge, skills and a never say die attitude.

Educating yourself is extremely important. You need to start reading books instead of watching TV and going to the pub with friends. Most people finish university and never pick up a book again. If you are not growing you are dying! Start attending property and business seminars, find your nearest networking event, meet new people. Remember your network is your net worth. It's not who you know, it's who knows you. You never know who you are going to meet at a seminar or networking event; it could be someone who can help you. The power of networking is amazing, sometimes you meet people who might not necessarily be useful to you but who might know someone with the tools and resources you are looking for. You only need one business deal, one opportunity, or to meet that one person and your whole life could change. Remember, never judge people on face value.

Chapter VI

Lease Options/Rent to Buy

What is a Lease Option?

No mortgage, No finance, No problem

Lease Option is one of the best and most powerful strategies in the property investing field. Lease option was first implemented in commercial property and is still widely used. The strategy works well for commercial properties so why not use it in the residential market too?

In a lease option, a motivated seller and the investor agree that, at any point in a specified option period for the given property, the buyer has the option of purchasing the property.

What does this mean? The price and option period to purchase the property is agreed at the beginning of the contract, e.g. the seller agrees to sell his house for £100,000 and the buyer has an option to buy it within 10 years' time. What does it all mean to the buyer? It means that the buyer can purchase the property any time within that 10-year period for £100,000. The beauty of it is that the buyer has an option to buy this property but not the obligation to purchase it. He can simply walk away when the option period ends.

Why would the seller give somebody an option to purchase his property for £100,000 if the property within 10 years' time could double in value, which will benefit the investor? There are many answers for these questions; the first reason would be that the buyer bought a property for £100,000 in 2005 and the property crash came in 2008; property prices went down in value and the house now is worth £70,000-£80,000. It would be nearly impossible to sell the property for the same price it was purchased for. This means that the owner is in negative equity right now; he/she wants to move somewhere else and maybe buy another house but he/she can't afford to pay 2 mortgages and doesn't want to rent or deal with any tenants, as there is no guarantee that the property would be let out or that maintenance issues wouldn't arise. If they sell the property for £70,000-£80,000, they would then have to come up with £20,000-£30,000 from their own money to pay off the remainder of the mortgage borrowed from the bank. Who would want to do that? It would be a complete waste of money.

Prior to the credit crunch, properties had doubled or tripled in some areas over the years, homeowners re mortgaged and borrowed a lot of money when their properties increased in value. Some banks would lend up to 125% on the value of their houses. When the property market crash came in 2008, property prices worldwide plummeted and many people were stuck with properties they could no longer afford. Some of them are still in negative equity.

Another reason could be that the property is worth £100,000 and the seller's mortgage is also £100,000. The seller needs to move overseas because they may have secured a new job over there or lost their job and can't keep up with the mortgage payments and they need to sell their house immediately, otherwise the house will be repossessed and their credit score will be affected for 7-10 years and they will not be able to get any loan or mortgage within that time. If the seller has little or no equity in their property, they can neither sell to cash buyers nor drop the price sufficiently with estate agents to attract any interest. Even if somehow they find somebody that will pay full market value for the property it usually takes 3-6 months to sell. Sometimes the sale can fall through because the buyer's mortgage was rejected or someone is stuck in a chain, meaning that he/she can't buy a new house until he/she sells their previous house.

The only option for the seller is to do a lease option where the investor has an option to purchase the property for a set price, look after the property maintenance, pay the seller's mortgage and any insurance or ground rent/service charges so the seller can then move on with their life. If the seller no longer needs to worry about the mortgage payments and the maintenance of the property, wouldn't it be the same as selling the property? The buyer can either live in the property, rent the property for more than the cost of the mortgage payment, so therefore a profit is made every month. Another option could be to sell the property for a higher price than agreed with the seller any time within the option period. But again, the contract needs to be designed in a way that you are allowed to transfer the option to somebody else. So if you like the sound of this strategy and it's something you would like to do, make sure you get the contract drafted properly by a solicitor that specialises in lease options and has done these kinds of deals and transactions before. If you go to the first local solicitor in your area, they might not know anything about lease options and could tell you it can't be done, it's like going to the GP doctor to do your heart surgery – you need someone that specializes in property.

There are people who say: "I can't invest in property, my credit score is very low, I have missed payments, the banks will not lend to me or my credit score is good but I don't have enough money for deposit at the moment." With Lease Option you don't need a good credit score or deposit! You can invest in property without taking any mortgages. If you bought a house and you took a mortgage and you put a 25% deposit upfront, you might think now I am an owner, I own a house. No you don't, the bank owns it! If you disagree, stop paying your mortgage for 3-5 months and you will see who owns it.

Isn't a Lease Option the same as if you bought the house? It's even better because you don't have to take a mortgage and put down a deposit on the property – the seller has already done it for you, and if the property goes up in value you will benefit in the same way as if you purchased the property. Guess how many lease options you can acquire? As many as you want! Unlimited!

With the standard Buy to Let product, do you think banks will allow you to buy unlimited number of properties? They won't; you will have to think outside the box and come up with something more creative to buy more. What is a liability to someone could be an asset for you! In a typical Lease Option scenario, we have a seller that has a mortgage, but they don't want their mortgage anymore and you want a mortgage and you can't get a mortgage. It comes to a simple conclusion – you take over their mortgage payments, although the mortgage still remains in the seller's name!

A win-win situation where everyone is happy.

You need to pay for the option-to-buy property – guess how much it is? It's a pound. One pound!! Isn't that great? Buying a house for a pound? The reason for this is that the nominal price needs to be paid in order for the seller to grant you an option to buy; otherwise the contract would be invalid. We have done many of these one pound deals during our time in property. We are not only getting cash flow from these properties every single month but also capital appreciation. There are many different ways of structuring Lease Option deals – you can extend the option period or you can share the profit or equity with the seller and more. In Lease Option, it's all about the terms. At our live seminars and coaching programs we will discuss in detail the advanced strategies that would allow you to maximise your rental profits. We will show you how to find lease options deals and how to negotiate these deals. Go to our website www.masterthepropertygame.com to check out our upcoming seminars and coaching programs.

What is Rent to Buy?

If you have control over a property either with Lease Option or mortgage, you can grant an option to your tenant to buy the property from you sometime in the future at a fixed price. One of the reasons why you might do that is to treat it as an exit strategy, so your tenant now has a sense of ownership and they will look after the maintenance of the property by themselves instead of bothering you. If the property that you bought is trashed or your previous tenants destroyed it, or it just needs some work to be done to it, this is the perfect strategy to use instead of you spending £1000s on renovating it. Your tenant will do that at their own pace and budget as they know one day it will be their house and the work they do could bring up the house value. Tenant buyers, by having an option to purchase your property, will pay you some cash in exchange for granting them an option to have it one day, and this time it won't be £1 like with a lease option. Now you are in a control and you can ask for fee of a few thousand pounds, plus you can charge rent that's slightly higher than the market value. There are a lot of people renting properties as they can't get a mortgage or don't have enough money for a deposit. When they pay you extra rent every month, you can offset some of the money towards their deposit if they choose to buy it in the future. Rent to Buy strategy helps the buyer to get on the property ladder immediately. There are a lot of investors that can't stand the hassle of their tenants. If they knew about this strategy, they would have a perfect tenant paying them a lot of money to get the option, looking after the maintenance of the property and paying above market rent.

Double Settlement

This strategy is very powerful when implemented correctly. What is double settlement? This strategy is used when, for example, you negotiate a discount on the property and you can sell it for much more than you would be paying for it. The beauty of it is that you don't need to purchase the property first in order to complete such a transaction, so even if you have bad credit history or don't have money for a deposit, you can still make a big chunk of cash. All you have to do is to find a buyer that will pay more for the house than you negotiated, connect them with the seller and let them complete the transaction. But before you do the connection, you need to have the right agreements signed with the vendor that will protect your interest. Everything needs to run efficiently and smoothly. The buyer should be found within a few days because usually when somebody sells their house with a discount, they expect the transaction to be completed ASAP, most commonly within 28 days. That is why it's important to look for the buyers who are interested in getting a little bit of discount instead of buying their house at the full market value before you run your marketing campaign.

You need to go to networking events, ask friends, family, hairdressers, shop owners, doctors, etc., so you have people lined up. There are some more advanced strategies you can implement to get buyers begging you for deals that we teach at our seminars and coaching programs. You need to have your own solicitors that can do the transaction very quickly. You also need buyers ready with cash or a decision in principle from the bank to purchase the property, as the last thing you want is for the sale to fall through because the buyer's mortgage was rejected by the lender. There is no time for this kind of mistake, so you need to make sure you check everything with the buyer before connecting them with the seller.

Example:
Price Negotiated: £80,000
House value: £120,000
Buyer's purchase price: £100,000

Once you have the right contract in place, the seller will receive the £80,000 that was agreed between you and them, and the difference between the price negotiated and the purchase price will be paid straight to your bank account. In this case, it is a value of £20,000 – not a bad sum of money, is it? This is what we are talking about – you don't need money to invest in property! Once you have the right knowledge and know what kind of contracts to use, you can become financially free very quickly with no money, no deposit and poor credit history!

Delayed Completion

Delayed completion is a variation on an option where you can exchange on a property, thereby negating the risk of refurb costs. You will basically own the property once exchanged but the completion could be delayed or you can pay for it in instalments over a period of many years. In a place like Scotland where lease option is not allowed, 'Delayed Completion' is a very common strategy to use because it's similar and the Scottish law allows it. Delayed completion can be used like it's a lease option, the only difference is that once you exchange you become obligated to complete.

Case Study 2 - Lease Option
Noble Street, Great Harwood, Blackburn

Property type: 2 Bedroom terraced house
Freehold/Leasehold: Leasehold 887 years,
Ground Rent: £0 absent freeholder
Option Period: 10 years
Option Fee: £1
Option Price: £53,188
House Value: 62,000

Monthly Mortgage Payment: £110.70 (Interest Only)
Agreed Rent: £400
Cash Flow: £289.30

Chapter VII

HMO and Rent to Rent

What is HMO?

A HMO is a house in multiple occupations, where you share a part of the accommodation with a group of people who are not related. Basically, tenants rent a room and share a bathroom, kitchen and a living room.

Rules and Regulations

Different rules and regulations apply to different countries and different councils, so before you acquire your first HMO you need to check the requirements with the particular local council. Generally, the regulations set by the councils are for the tenants' safety. The more unrelated tenants in a house, the higher the risk. You sometimes can have many personalities and cultures under one roof, especially in places like London. We had one tenant that liked to have a drink every now and again. There was one particular occasion when he had a bit to drink and got a bit peckish; it happened to be midnight. He fell asleep with the oven on and if it wasn't for the smoke alarms the house would have been burnt to down to nothing. Here's an example of why you not only need referencing checks but background checks too.

This was the beginning of our journey in property and we can safely say we did not do well with our tenant selection in that instance.

It's important that you make sure that you have valid insurance in place suitable for HMOs, Most HMOs require fire doors, smoke alarms, carbon monoxide detectors, gas and boiler safety checks every year. A fire extinguisher should also be provided, along with a first aid kits and a fire blanket. You will also need to provide PAT safety stickers for all electrical appliances.

What is Rent to Rent and How Does it Work?

Rent to Rent is another brilliant strategy that can supercharge your cash flow. You can make a lot of money from the property without even owning it. The property is leased by yourself from the owner of the property. The rent paid by yourself to the owner is guaranteed even during void periods. You make your money by renting each room individually.

The Rent to Rent strategy is designed to target professionals and students that are looking to pay less rent than renting a studio or flat alone they don't want to worry about paying bills so we always include it in the rent payment, the housemate would pay the same amount every single month and some like to house share mainly for the social element.

You need to have the correct contracts in place. You could be breaking the law if you don't. The contracts need to permit subletting and the landlord needs to be fully aware of your actions.

It's a business; the landlord has piece of mind for a few years and their rent is guaranteed every single month. You do the dirty work or get it taken care of, and make some good money by managing the property and renting it room by room.

When I say dirty work, it doesn't mean that you have to do it all; this isn't what property is all about. You hire people who are more skilled when it comes to getting their hands dirty and dealing with tenancy issues so you can focus on sourcing more and more properties that will bring you thousands of pounds per month. Some people choose to take care of the management themselves and do all the £10 jobs repairing toilets, assembling furniture, doing viewings, etc. As mentioned, we started out doing just about everything and it was not something we enjoyed. Having everything systemised and centralised is the key; the last thing you want is to create a job for yourself.

The Rent to Rent strategy requires very little start-up capital. You can create great cash flow and the money made can be used to re-invest into other ventures, even your first Buy to Let.

Why Location Is the Key

Location for the Rent to Rent strategy is very important as the rent is guaranteed to the landlord and there is not much margin for error and empty rooms could be very costly.

Professionals and students will be looking to live as close to their universities or their place of work as possible. Train stations and amenities should ideally be no more than a 15 minute walk from the property. There are exceptions if the property is located close to hospitals, factories or warehouses but you still need to check the rental demand prior. We have one property quite a distance away from a train station. Luckily it's close to amenities and a hospital. This property was a bargain and the numbers work very well; surprisingly it brings us the most money on a monthly basis. The property has 2 bathrooms and huge garden, which attracts tenants. Before we took this property, we had to make sure the rental demand was very good in the area; we did not want problems finding tenants. You can do a simple test by placing a dummy advert online to check if there is any interest in the area.

Due Diligence

Before you lease a property, you need to make sure that the numbers stack up. Do your calculations before you take on any property; it's imperative to make sure you can profit from it. We always know how much each property will bring us roughly, before we put any offers forward. You need to know how much you can afford to offer in order for the deal to work for you, taking into consideration bills, maintenance and outsourcing fees. For example, we have a general rule that we follow; the property needs be within a 15 minute walk from the station with a cash flow of at least £600. If it doesn't meet our criteria, we simply won't take on the property. You need to know how much council tax will cost each month: gas and electric, water rates, cleaner, internet, maintenance and outsourcing. Does the property require any work? Sometimes the landlord may find it very difficult to rent the property in the current condition it's in, and if we can get the property for the right price, we are more than happy to do a little bit of work to get it up to a rentable standard. Is the property furnished or unfurnished? Do you need to provide furniture?

Everything mentioned above needs to be included in your calculations, so check your cash flow and return on investment. To check the room prices in across the UK, we use Gumtree, Spareroom or Easyroommate to help with our calculations.

Sourcing and Managing the Right Tenants

There are many different ways of sourcing tenants. You can market and carry out viewings yourself or you can outsource the job to individuals or letting agents. Agents tend to charge a larger fee, but they are thorough with their checks and generally bring good quality tenants. Having said that, we would suggest finding somebody that wants to make a little bit of extra cash and simply get them to duplicate your skills and techniques. You'll end up saving a lot of money and the person you employ will be chuffed with the extra cash earned.

It's very important to reference check every prospective tenant that you rent to; you need to make sure that any tenant from a non-European country has a valid visa. It's a criminal offence to rent to anybody not allowed in the country and you could receive a hefty fine. Make sure you check last 3 months' worth of bank statements and payslips, a copy of their ID and previous landlords and work references.

Always make sure you take a deposit for a room just in case of any damages to the property or their room. In England, the deposit needs to be protected with an accredited government scheme. You are liable for up to 3 times the deposit plus legal costs if the tenant chooses to take action against an unprotected deposit. All tenants should all be under 6 month contract. It is a law abiding document that you will need to provide in court, in case of an eviction. It's very important before you take a new property to know what sort of tenants you will be renting to.

You can't mix students with professionals or builders with doctors or office workers. They have a different mind-set and different living habits. You will run into problems, and the last thing you want is four good tenants moving after 6 months because of one bad one.

Case Study 3 - Rent to Rent
Selworthy Road, London
HMO acquired 12th June 2015

Property Type: End Terrace House, 6 beds, 2 baths
Lease: £1800 per month

Rent from tenants:
Room 1: £420
Room 2: £550
Room 3: £580
Room 4: £500
Room 5: £550
Room 6: £370
Total: £2970
Bills: £330
Net monthly cash flow: £840

Chapter VIII

Buy to Sell vs Buy to Let

Buy to Sell

Firstly, I am going to discuss making money using Buy to Sell. Buy to Sell is a strategy used when an investor has intentions of making a large sum of money. These types of property investors are not interested in letting and earning cash flow every month, they are simply in it for the big bucks. This is a very lucrative strategy but at the same time it can be very risky; I would not advise using this strategy as a property newbie. This strategy requires experience, knowledge and a huge appetite for risk but as they say, "More risk more reward."

We buy to hold for the long term, but having said that when sourcing properties there is a chance you may come across a few that may not reach your rental requirements. The rental rates in that particular area may not be sufficient enough to cover your mortgage or your desired cash flow amount. We specialise in multi lets but in some cases the area or location might not be right. Instead of walking away due to rental terms, the property may have the potential to be sold at a higher price to maybe a first-time buyer or potentially an investor that's happy with 5-10% below market value (BMV).

Ideally, when buying with the intention to sell, you want to purchase a property that you can add value to. Firstly, the more value you add the better, and secondly, you want to be able to purchase the property at a discount, or in other words, below market value. If you can achieve both of these, you are on to a winner.

Discount – when buying with the intention to sell on, the rule of thumb is that you need to purchase at 20-25% below the true market value, depending on the area. This is the discount you need to gain even more out of the deal; the discount would ideally cover the purchase costs, sales costs, and holding costs.

Numbers – you have to know your numbers! This is so crucial when it comes to buying to sell. Is there a decent enough bundle of cash waiting at the end of it all? After all the hard work, sleepless nights, blood, sweat and tears, the last thing you want is to walk away with a tiny profit, no profit or even worse, a loss. It's all about the numbers, which leads me on to the next section. Timing – once your timing is off, it affects the numbers; it's that simple. Ideally you need a trustworthy and skilled power team. This would include builders, plumbers, electricians, painters and decorators, even bridgers if you plan to go down that route. Everybody has to work in tangent and there has to be a plan that everybody sticks to. Preparation is key! Remember: fail to prepare, prepare to fail. There are tons of cowboys out there, so beware! They can cost you a lot of time which would have a direct effect on the numbers, i.e. your holding costs (monthly interest payments on your mortgage, insurance, council tax) which all add up, which would then eat into your bottom line, i.e. your lump sum at the end. As we all know, time is money!

Estate Agent – Ideally you want to try and minimise the amount of time you are holding the property for and the time taken to sell your property, which partly depends on the estate agent you use. It's vital that you select the right estate agent. You want to ideally use an agent you have built a relationship with and who has a good track record, as they will try harder to sell the property because it's yours. I wouldn't recommend trying to negotiate too hard with regards to their commission – if anything you should offer them a bonus if they sell fast. This will give them even more of an incentive.

Knowing the market – again this is one that ties in with the last 3 things I mentioned. It's all about the ease of sale, and one HUGE factor could be reliance on what the market is doing at the time you are trying to sell. If the market is static or declining, then you may have difficulty selling, which means you would be holding on to the property a lot longer than you first planned to. On top of that, in order to sell, you may have to lower your asking price. You need to take the market conditions into account before using this strategy.

Focus on quality – now it's not all about buying the cheapest materials and getting the property refurbished to a bog standard; you want to make the property appealing. Not only is this ethical but the property will sell a lot quicker at the price you would like it to sell for. When you buy a property BMV there may be a chance the property will be old, and dated with tired décor. If you try and sell it on straight away with a green bathroom with yellow tiles and a living room with flowery wallpaper, you might have trouble. In addition, agents will value it at pretty much the same price you bought it for, and prospective buyers will try and buy it cheaper, too. To attract a first-time buyer, for example, you need to make sure the property looks attractive. Remember, first impressions are everything, and it's amazing what one lick of paint and a tidy up can do. Domestic improvement is also an investment because if you think about it you are adding value and you have to spend money to make money. It's definitely worthwhile. Wherever you can add value, why not add a bathroom or a kitchen, give the garden a tidy up or add some air fresheners for when you do viewings. It also may be worth spending a bit of money on dressing the property or even leasing higher quality furniture.

For example, you earn £40,000 from one property after 3 months of refurbishment; that's more than most people earn per year in their job! Imagine doing 2, 3 or 4 a year or have multiple deals/developments going on at any one time. What could this do to your lifestyle? Your family's lifestyle? If you have a reliable team that you don't have to keep an eye on, how much time would this free

Buy to Let

Buy to Let, the more common of the two strategies, is where you purchase a property with the sole intention to rent it out to earn an income after all expenses. A Buy to Let mortgage is specifically designed for this purpose. This is a residual/passive income strategy where ideally after all expenses you would look to pocket a minimum of £200 per month or £2400 per annum. It does not seem like much at a glance, but Buy to Let investors don't usually have one property; they intend to have a portfolio which is described in the dictionary as 'a range of investments held by a person or organisation.' So, to clarify, let's say a person in this case had 15 properties each producing a monthly profit of £200. The person who owns these 15 properties would receive a monthly income of £3000 per month and £36000 per annum.

The same monthly income you could get from 15 single lets can be achieved with just 3 to 4 HMOs. This is more than the average person makes from their 9-5 job working hard for somebody else.

Another advantage with Buy to Let is that when the property goes up in value, you can pull your money out completely tax free! How? By refinancing. If you have purchased a Buy to Let property in the right market conditions, as soon as you have reached 6 months of owning that property you will be able to go to the bank and they will be able to give you a new mortgage based on the value of your property in the UK. I (Shane) bought a property in London in 2013, which was the right time to buy as the property has appreciated in value.

Not only do you now potentially have enough for a deposit on a new property, you still hold the asset with the additional debt from refinancing being covered by the tenant. Furthermore, as it's a form of borrowing, it's completely tax-free! Again, this is a perfect example of leveraging through property and this is why we prefer buying to hold rather than buying to sell.

Just like buying to sell, buying to let does have risks, risks such as bad tenants, long voids, change in government policy, over-leveraging, drop in rental rates and/or demand. If you cannot meet the conditions of your mortgage repayments then the bank will repossess your property.

There are many things you need to consider when purchasing in order to minimise the risk:

Numbers – as mentioned in the last section, the numbers are just as important. Does the investment stack up after landlord insurance, property management fees, service charge/ground rent, leasehold building, boiler, heating, drainage cover, etc? These are all the things amateur investors forget to consider and, as a general rule of thumb, you would ideally want to have a NET cash flow of £200 after all the expenses listed above. Buy to Let lenders usually want rent to cover 125% of the mortgage repayments and most ask for a 25% deposit upfront, or more. There is the odd company that asks for 20% but we would advise shopping around or sourcing a reliable mortgage broker. Location – the location is a crucial factor and will be important in any strategy involving property investment. You need to make sure the property is located in an area where people actually want to live. Is it safe? Is it close to local facilities, amenities, transport links, any regeneration happening in the area? These questions might come across simplistic, but they are probably the most important aspects to consider if you want to become a success at property investing.

In most cases, people tend to invest in property close to where they live, even though I believe a property is an asset no matter which part of the country it is in. With my experience, I believe it is best to invest as close to you as your budget will allow you to. The advantages for this is that you are likely to know the market better than anywhere else, especially if you have other properties close by and you have lived in a particular area for a number of years and can spot the kind of property and location that will do well. You can also keep tabs on the property if you feel you need to; at least the option is there to visit the property with ease every now and again.

Features – features could be anything from fire places, high ceilings, flooring to even the type of furniture you dress the property with. It's all about quality. Provide a quality property then you will attract quality tenants. Not only that but you can also boost your rental prices. This is one way that it is still possible to see a more secure and higher return on your capital invested. If you can add value to a property immediately, then it gives you a larger margin of safety on your money invested. Remember it's all about adding value where you can.

Size and amount of bedrooms – the size and the number of bedrooms in the property is another important factor to consider. Not only if you intend to rent to a family but if you wish to rent out the property as a House of Multiple Occupancy (HMO), whereby you rent rooms individually, then the room sizes become even more important. Where possible, you want to fit a double bed, chest of drawers, wardrobe and bedside table comfortably in the room, leaving a decent amount of space to actually move around in. The number of rooms speaks for itself; the more rooms you have in a property the more it should rent for. There is one thing to look out for; if you acquire a 6-bedroom property please be aware that this property will be very difficult to rent to a family as a single let. Properties of this size and magnitude are more suitable as HMOs.

If done correctly, the Buy to Let strategy can be very lucrative. It can provide you with an income that would replace most jobs which in turn will free up your most valued asset which is time. Over time, as each one of your properties appreciates in value, you are becoming wealthier which then provides more options. You can refinance, sell up or pass down your portfolio to your next generation and start a legacy. The choice is yours, and all these choices are possible by choosing to become a Buy to Let property investor.

Chapter I X

Auctions

What is an Auction?

An auction is a place in which investors bid openly against one another and properties are sold to the highest bidder. Auctions are open to the public to ensure a wide range of bids, and sometimes properties at auction can fetch surprisingly high prices. The auction is managed by an auctioneer, a person who keeps an eye on the bidding process and determines the ultimate winner. Usually the seller will set up a minimum sell price to ensure that the property is not sold for less than he/she is willing to sell for. If the reserve price is not met, the property will be withdrawn by the auctioneer.

Due Diligence

Properties are listed by an auctioneer, and can be found in an auction catalogue. You can request such a catalogue to be sent to you by post, it's a good idea to check all the details for each lot for thorough due diligence. The description of each property will be in the catalogue along with guide prices.

The guide price is just an indication of what the property's reserve price is, based on the vendor's expectations, and not necessarily the price at which the property will sell for. Sold prices achieved could be higher or lower than the guide price; most of the time the properties are not visited by the auctioneer and the details are very limited. But at least you will get an idea of what sort of properties are available.

You need to take into consideration that these properties are on an auction for a reason and some could be un-mortgageable due to some sort of defect or structural problem. Most houses with these problems are bought by the builders and developers.

If you win a bid at an auction in the UK, you usually have to come up with 10 % of the purchase price on the same day. In other countries this may vary; it's imperative that you check with your local auction house. The next step after the 10% deposit has been paid is you then have 28 days to carry out legal searches, a conveyancing process and arrange the rest of the finance in order to complete. It's very important to have all finances ready before you start bidding as 28 days is a very short time, and it's very hard to complete with a standard BTL mortgage unless you carry out a surveyor valuation beforehand

and get your mortgage pre-approved. If you don't have enough cash, an alternative option is bridging finance, used by most builders and developers that buy houses at auctions. You can get approved quickly but you need to bear in mind that bridging loans are very expensive – 1-3% per month, so there is a lot of risk involved in it. You need to make sure that you have a few exit strategies in place and you know your numbers. With an auction, there is a lot of cash involved and even if you take a bridging loan and later on you struggle to get a mortgage, you can go bust, so you need to be very vigilant and have an astute plan of action prior.

Never buy any property without seeing it beforehand! You need to know what sort of condition the property is in; it could be completely trashed which could cost you a lot of money, and might not be worth the hassle. Make sure that before you attend an auction you know everything about the house you are looking to purchase: the area, rental demand, how much rent you can achieve if you plan to hold and, most importantly, the value of the property. Call a couple of local estate agents to find out how much the houses sell for in the area, check sold prices and the land registry to make sure that there are no charges on the property or any restrictions. The last thing you want is to find out that there is a life tenant occupying the property, which means that they can live in the property until they pass away. Go and see the property. I would suggest obtaining a surveyor's valuation before bidding. It is better to lose £500 for the valuation than thousands of pounds for getting the value wrong or to find out that there are structural problems which could turn out to be very costly, or that the house is un-mortgageable. If you decide not to spend money on a valuation, it would be wise to view the property with an experienced builder, for obvious reasons. If you have just started your property journey, we wouldn't advise buying at an auction. Property auctions are for professional investors and developers that have a lot of cash and tons of experience

Controlling Emotions

Controlling emotions is key in business. Know your maximum bidding price and never under any circumstances go above that. Work out your numbers before you attend an auction. Avoid bidding wars; know your maximum and stick to it!

Don't get drawn in by the amateurs; they will over-bid as they do not know the true value of the property. You know your maths, so don't get involved.

When to Bid and Put Offers and Why

Never be the first person to start bidding; let your competition do the hard work first then you enter. There are two cheeky ways of winning over your competition: You can call the auction house before the auction date and check if you can put in an offer before, there are a lot of properties withdrawn before the auction takes place; or you can also wait until the end of the auction day and check all the properties where the reserve price hasn't been met, then speak to an auctioneer and put your offers in for the property you would like to purchase. In some cases you can even place an offer less than the most recent bid and still get accepted.

Chapter X

Get Started and Master the Property Game

Don't wait to buy property; buy property and wait. There's no better time to start than now. If I could start all over again, I would firstly invest in myself and my property education. Seeing that you have bought this book and you have gotten this far, it shows a level of resiliency as you have not just invested the money in yourself, you have invested the time. I (Shane) learned the hard way initially by making mistakes and losing money – a lot of money; it was a very expensive lesson to learn. Why not learn from someone who has been successful in property and has made all the mistakes? They can guide you through and lead you away from the many pitfalls that come with property investing. Damian, on the other hand, learnt from mentors when starting out in property, which eliminated the errors and expensive mistakes. Remember, once you invest in yourself, the knowledge you obtain will stay with you forever. You can have the houses, the money, the cars and the rest of the fancy luxuries taken away from you but you can never have your knowledge taken away.

Damian and I have easily spent over £60,000 on our own personal development and education. We are always looking to enhance our skills, knowledge and grow as individuals. As Jim Rohn says "You are either growing or you're dying." There are many ways to learn and grow; there are books, audio/video seminars, live seminars, coaching programmes, home study courses, networking events, etc. The question is not how much will it cost you to invest, but how much will it cost you not to invest. Remember, you are your biggest asset and your potential is unlimited. Pour your wallet into your mind and your mind will pour 10x the investment back into your wallet.

What other tools do you need to get started on mastering the property game?

You need a **strong positive mental attitude**; business and investing is 85% mind-set and 15% skillset. Don't get me wrong – skillset is very important as mentioned but without a strong mental attitude your skills mean nothing. To be a true success you need to have the right attitude and self-belief that you can achieve anything you put your mind to. Most people on the outside think you have to be a wizard or Einstein. They believe it's all about knowledge and different techniques when this is really not the case. Perseverance is the key.

You need to be **coachable**; the most dangerous place to be is being that person that believes that they know it all. Most people believe that they know it all as soon as they leave university and then never ever pick up a book again for the rest of their life. Part of being coachable is being a good listener, and somebody that knows it all tends to talk more than they listen. When you listen, you learn. As investors we have to be problem-solvers at times, and to solve problems we have to try and take in as much information as possible to give us the best chance of solving the problem. Even to this day, with all we have achieved, we continue to invest in our personal development and still spend money on coaching and mentoring.

Self-discipline – self-discipline is a trait every business man or woman needs. We are effectively our own boss, so it's easy to make excuses and try and justify them to ourselves. We all need to have a strong enough reason why we have chosen this path, and it has to be a reason bigger than ourselves. Why? Because it's easy to quit on ourselves, but if we all have a strong reason why, that should be more than enough to bring us through. You need to be able to push yourself to your maximum limit, and even past your limits and way outside your comfort zone, because in your comfort zone is where success lies. You may have to sacrifice less money for more money in the long run, less time for more time, less sleep for more sleep, less relaxing Sunday afternoons for eventually everyday feeling like a Sunday afternoon. You cannot change your life overnight but changing your direction and small daily habits will compound and change your life over time for the better.

Persistence and resiliency; Property is not easy. If it were, we would all be cash rich property investors. A lot of people face their first obstacle or suffer a minor setback and they run the opposite way. They give up far too easily, probably just short of achieving their goals. Remember everything you ever wanted is on the other side of fear. If other people have found a way to do it, there is no reason why you can't achieve the same. You will come across many negative people along the way, 'dream stealers,' but every human being on this earth is entitled to their own opinion. Opinions aren't facts, don't let someone else's opinion determine your future. If you are buying into somebody's opinion you are buying into their lifestyle along with their way of thinking.

The Purpose of this Book

The purpose of this book is to give you insights and elevate your level of understanding with regard to property investing and all the strategies that come with it. The main aim is to educate and inspire ¬– educate you on what is possible and inspire you to make a change going forward.

We have kept the techniques and strategies fairly basic because we do not want to overload you with information, especially if you are new to property investing. The last thing you want is information overload. This is just the tip of the iceberg of what we could teach you on a personal basis. Having said that there is enough information in this book for anybody to go out and take considerable action. Remember knowledge is not power – it's potential power. It's only power if you put your knowledge into practice.

We really hope that you have enjoyed reading this book, and that you have taken value from it. We hope to educate and inspire as many people as possible, and we truly believe that having the ability to share information and at the same time inspire others is our purpose. So now it is up to you to take action.

If you would like to watch an exclusive interview with Donald Trump's right-hand man George Ross and you would like to learn more about property investing, please visit our website: www.masterthepropertygame.com

Follow us on social media:
https://www.facebook.com/DamianSlominskiOfficial
https://www.facebook.com/Shanepwatson

Acknowledgements

I would like to acknowledge the following: Firstly, my partner, soul mate and rock Lauren Wolsey for always being there and supporting me throughout. She also helped edit the book! My illustrious business partners, investors, co-author and good friends, Damian Slominski (co-author), Leiam Gordon, Aaron D Samuels and Michael Craney. The person that first exposed me to the Rent to Rent strategy over Christmas dinner 2013 – my brother Shai Watson. My supportive "tell it how it is" sister Shakira Watson and my baby sister Tushana. My day-to-day motivator and the person that first exposed me to property investing at the age of 19, Ansel Sobers. Top-notch friends, as well as creative graphic designers, Reiss Butler and Jamie Honor. My fellow business partner, good friend, property investor and funny guy, Reese Withey. Sam, Teshan and Nicolle Williams – for all your help in the day to day running of my property business. Ludlow Thompson Estate Agency for the many property deals and putting their trust in me from the start. My property coaches and mentors John Lee, Vincent Wong and Florence NG. My personal development and life mentors George Ross, Robert Kyosaki, Les Brown, Jim Rohn and Eric Worre. Last but not least my parents for creating and raising me.

I would like to acknowledge my co-author and good friend, Shane Watson, business partners and investors Wojciech Wojtulewicz, Josh Bardsley, Michael Brodie, Romain Neyses, Kieran Ekeledo and Zohra Benjamin. My best friend, Marika Bialek, thank you for all the support, encouragement and belief, for always being there for me even during the tough times in my business career where everything was going wrong and I could still count on you. My sister, Marika Slominska, for giving me the opportunity to move to the UK. My property mentors and coaches, John Lee, Vincent Wong and Florence Ng for all the advice and help. My Forex mentor, Hither Mann, for teaching me and showing the importance of psychology in trading and business life. Our book architect Naval Kumar who keeps me accountable and helps me to put everything together, without you it would take us years to complete this book. My mum for showing me and letting me understand why I should invest into property. My dad for exposing me to business from a young age – I did not realise before how important a lesson it was for me, and now I am sure that because of him I always wanted to be a business owner and not an employee. My personal development and life mentors, George Ross, Les Brown, T. Harv Eker, Robert Kiyosaki, Sharon Lechter, Tony Robbins, Raymond Aaron, Bob Proctor, Dr. John Demartini, and Nick Vujicic. I would also like to thank J.T. Foxx, for giving me a lot of opportunities and connecting me with the right people.

Printed in Great Britain
by Amazon